16

japanese food made easy

fiona uyema

japanese food made easy

fiona uyema

MERCIER PRESS
Irish Publisher – Irish Story

This book is dedicated to my husband Gilmar and my beautiful boys Scott and Matthew.

contents

chicken

beef, pork & lamb

fish & seafood

vegetarian

acknowledgements

A huge thanks to my husband Gilmar for his never-ending belief in me and for being so supportive throughout the making of this book.

To all my family and friends, thanks for encouraging me over the years and giving me the confidence to share my passion for Japanese food. A special thanks to my sisters and mother, Ann, for being on-call babysitters, recipe testers and critics whenever I needed them.

Thanks to all my Japanese friends who have taught me so much about Japanese culture and food since I embarked on my first journey to Japan back in 2000.

Thanks to all the team at Mercier Press. A special thanks to Sarah and Sharon for believing in my vision for this book.

Thanks to Rob, Orla, Sarah and Olga for working so hard on the photo shoot, which was filled with laughter and good memories. It was an unforgettable and invaluable learning experience for me.

Finally, thanks to all of you for supporting me over the last few years. Please bring this book into your kitchens and let Japanese cooking become part of your life. You'll never look back.

Fiona x

introduction

I'll always be grateful to Japan for two reasons: it's where I met my husband Gilmar and where I found my passion for food.

After growing up on a farm in a small rural village in County Tipperary, Ireland, I moved to Dublin to study Japanese in college. I was intrigued by everything Japanese, but it was only by living in Japan for three years that I truly experienced the different aspects of its culture and learned how to speak the language with confidence and fluency.

During my college year abroad I stayed with a Japanese homestay family in a city called Takasaki, located in the heart of Japan, 100 kilometres from Tokyo. In the evenings I would sit at the kitchen table chatting to my homestay mother and watching her prepare that evening's meal in her small Japanese kitchen, where the most important appliance is the electric rice cooker. Most Japanese kitchens have small electric grills rather than conventional ovens. The food was always delicious and I was surprised how easily she could prepare a vast range of dishes from scratch with minimal fuss. I became fascinated with Japanese food and everything about it, and found myself researching terms such as 'umami' so I could understand the foundations of Japanese cuisine. It was through this experience of living with a Japanese family in Takasaki that I became fully immersed in learning about Japanese cooking and, without realising it, began my journey to becoming a Japanese home-cook.

A major benefit of the Japanese diet is that it is one of the healthiest in the world. It is low in fat, with little use of butter or other dairy products – tofu, seaweed and dark-

green vegetables are the main sources of calcium. It's high in good protein through daily consumption of fish and soya-based products, and contains many foods high in antioxidants which also aid digestion, such as green tea and miso.

After observing the way Japanese people eat, I realised that culture and lifestyle also play an important role in their healthy diet. For example, the concept of balance is important at mealtimes, so a selection of dishes from the different food groups are cooked in a variety of ways and served at each meal.

It was while living in a beautiful city in Japan called Kanazawa that I met my husband, Gilmar. We were introduced to each other by mutual friends and it wasn't long before we were inseparable, sharing our passion for food and Japan. Our surname, Uyema, is pronounced ou-yay-ma and comes from the Okinawa Prefecture, a chain of beautiful tropical islands off the south of Japan. It should be spelt Uema, but when Gilmar's grandparents emigrated from Okinawa to Brazil the letter 'y' was somehow added to the name; possibly to make it easier to pronounce, or perhaps it was an administrative error. Like thousands of other Japanese and Okinawans in the early 1900s, Gilmar's grandparents moved to Brazil for a better life and, once there, they set up their own Japanese food business.

Okinawa is well known for having one of the longest life expectancies in the world, which is mostly attributed to the low-fat diet and the Okinawan way of living. There is a saying from Okinawa – *Hara hachi bu* – which means eat until you are 80 per cent full. Adopting this principle avoids overeating and feeling overfull, as it takes time for food to travel to the stomach and alert the brain that it's 100 per cent full. I try to live by this saying.

When I returned to Ireland, over ten years ago, I wanted to cook Japanese food at home, but it was difficult to find some of the key ingredients, which were not as widely available and reasonably priced as they are today. Then, a few years later, I was diagnosed with ovarian cancer and turned to the Japanese diet for comfort. During my chemo treatment I was in hospital for three months and I was horrified by the standard of food there. I knew that the Japanese diet would provide me with food packed with goodness that would help with my recovery, so every evening my husband came to the hospital with a Japanese bento packed especially for me. I can't tell you how much I looked forward to this and

how it helped me to get through a really tough time. Thankfully, my chemo treatment was successful and I returned to work the following year.

By then, my passion and appreciation for Japanese food had strengthened and I continued to integrate it more and more into my daily diet when I cooked at home. But with cancer, obesity and dietary-related health problems on the increase in Ireland and across the world, I also wanted to share my recipes and encourage people to try them at home, as I truly believe that, by incorporating Japanese food into their diet, people can live healthier lives. When I took a year off work for maternity leave with my first child, Scott, I had time to think about my cooking and the future. During my free time, I started to write a Japanese cooking blog and to give Japanese cooking classes, as well as demonstrating at food festivals and events across Ireland. I was energised by the extra work and the response I received from the Irish public.

When I was given the opportunity to write this book I had to pinch myself, as for me it was a dream come true. I want to bring you on the same exciting journey that I had when learning to cook Japanese food, by guiding you through the basics of Japanese cooking and giving you some of my favourite recipes, so that you can integrate this cuisine into your lifestyle and enjoy all the benefits that come with a Japanese diet!

The recipes I've included in this book are traditional Japanese recipes that I learned from friends, colleagues and neighbours while living in Japan. I've also included modern Japanese recipes which have been influenced by local ingredients available to me here in Ireland. Like most people these days, when I'm cooking at home I find that time constraints influence what's on the menu, so I've tried to make the recipes in this book as user-friendly as possible without compromising on the taste. I've also included notes and tips along with the recipes, to make your journey to becoming a Japanese home-cook as enjoyable as possible.

I hope you enjoy my book.

Fiona x

japanese food culture

While in Japan I worked in both elementary and junior high schools and got to see first-hand how food was part of each child's school education. In Japan it is common for each school to have their own nutritionist as part of the full-time working staff. The nutritionist plans the daily lunch menu for the children and the staff to ensure that they receive a well-balanced meal every day. The calories in each meal are counted to make sure that it's not above the recommended daily intake.

The children take turns helping to prepare and serve the lunch each day. This encourages them to learn about food and also to appreciate it from an early age. There is little tolerance for leftover food, so everyone is encouraged to try their best to leave no food behind. In Japanese homes leftover food is not thrown in the bin. If there is any food left from dinner, it is stored in the fridge and used the following day for breakfast or as part of a bento (a Japanese-style packed lunch; you can read more about Japan's bento culture on page 209).

A traditional Japanese home-cooked meal includes a bowl of rice accompanied by soup and several other communal dishes, including vegetables, fish and meat, to give a nutritionally balanced meal. In contrast to the home-cooked Japanese meal, there is also a type of meal called kaiseki, which is served in some higher-end restaurants in Japan. Kaiseki could be described as a fine-dining tasting menu with multiple courses. It's renowned for its beautiful presentation and close connection to nature. It could really be described as art.

Like Ireland, Japan has four distinct seasons and you can clearly see each of the seasons reflected in the food on the menus in restaurants and at home. This close connection between food and the natural world, with the use of local and seasonal ingredients to respect and maintain harmony with nature, is in essence the foundation of washoku (Japanese traditional cuisine).

In 2013 washoku became a topic of discussion around the world when it was added to UNESCO's 'intangible cultural heritage of humanity' list. This recognition has sparked an interest in Japanese food, with more and more people wanting to learn about it, and I hope this book goes some way towards helping them do so.

japanese dining etiquette

My homestay family taught me some important aspects of Japanese dining etiquette so that I didn't offend anyone without realising! Now I'm going to share these with you.

dining expressions

Japanese cuisine is closely associated with nature and showing respect for food is very important. At the beginning of every meal Japanese people give thanks for the food they're about to eat by saying 'itadaki-masu', and at the end of a meal they show their appreciation for the food just eaten by saying 'gochiso-sama'.

slurping

Most people are surprised that slurping is acceptable in Japan when eating certain types of food like hot noodle dishes such as ramen. The Japanese believe it makes the food taste nicer and also shows the chef that you are enjoying the food.

chopstick etiquette

When you are using chopsticks be careful NOT to do the following:

- Sit the chopsticks upright in a dish, as this is associated with death.
- Cross chopsticks: when you are not using chopsticks during a meal you should place them neatly alongside each other.
- Play with chopsticks, point at people with them or wave them around in your hand when talking. They should only be used for eating.

- Pick up food with chopsticks by sticking the chopstick into the food.
- Pass food using chopsticks: if you want to pass food to someone simply hand the dish to them.
- Use the end of the chopsticks that touched your mouth to take food from communal dishes. It is polite to turn your chopsticks around to take the food. However, in casual dining settings this is not necessary.

overuse of soy sauce (as table sauce)

In the West we tend to overuse soy sauce compared to Japanese people. Using too much soy sauce actually overpowers the flavour of the food so it's difficult to taste anything else. It's also offensive to the chef to overuse soy sauce, as it suggests that the dish isn't very flavoursome.

pouring drinks

When drinking with other people it is polite to wait for someone else to pour your drink and to be conscious to pour drinks for other people. If you would like your drink refilled, you can prompt someone by filling their drink and they'll in turn fill yours!

basic japanese ingredients

Large supermarkets and health stores stock a good selection of basic Japanese ingredients, and fishmongers often sell dried seaweed. Asian speciality stores, found all over Ireland, will have some of the more unusual ingredients. You can also order ingredients online. I have given a list of suppliers on page 216.

The following is a list of basic ingredients which you will need to begin cooking the recipes in this book.

rice (kome)

Japanese rice is a type of short-grain rice which sticks easily together when cooked, so it's perfect for making rice balls and sushi. It's also easier to eat with chopsticks! The difference between plain Japanese rice and sushi rice is that sushi rice is seasoned with sushi vinegar and used to make sushi.

noodles

Noodles play an important part in the Japanese diet. There's a variety of noodles used in Japanese cooking, including ramen, udon, soba and somen.

Ramen noodles are yellowish, thin and made from wheat. They are well known as one of the main ingredients in ramen broths.

Udon noodles are white, thick and made from wheat flour. This type of noodle is often served in a hot broth, but one of my favourite ways to eat udon noodles is covering them in leftover curry sauce.

Soba noodles are brown-grey, thin and made from buckwheat flour. They have a strong nutty flavour and can be served hot or cold. I love eating them topped with tempura.

Somen noodles are white, very thin and made from wheat. They're often served cold during the hot summer months.

soy sauce (shoyu)

Different countries produce different types of soy sauce. I prefer to use Japanese soy sauce when I'm cooking Japanese food (e.g. Kikkoman), as other types of soy sauce such as Chinese soy sauce will change the flavour of the dish. Japanese soy sauce is made by fermenting soy beans with wheat and brine.

tamari

This is a great alternative to soy sauce for people with gluten intolerance. Make sure the bottle states 'gluten-free' if you are gluten intolerant, as some brands may contain a little gluten. It's darker in colour and the taste is stronger than standard Japanese soy sauce.

rice vinegar (komezu)

Rice vinegar is mostly used to make sushi rice, Japanese salad dressings and some sauces. It has a very delicate taste compared to other vinegars.

sushi vinegar (sushizu)

You can make your own sushi vinegar with rice vinegar, sugar and salt. Alternatively you can buy it ready-made. I prefer to make mine from scratch as I can control the amount of sugar and salt (see recipe on page 172).

rice wine (sake)

The Japanese use sake the same way as we use wine when cooking in the West. It's an alcoholic drink made from rice. It adds a wonderful flavour to dishes and helps tenderise meat and fish.

sweet rice wine (mirin)

Mirin has a lower alcohol content than sake and is used only for cooking in Japan. It adds a nice sweet balance to Japanese dishes.

la yu – chilli-infused sesame oil

You'll find this on tables in restaurants as it's often added to dishes just before eating to add a spicy flavour.

sesame oil

Sesame oil is often used in Japanese cooking to give extra flavour.

sugar

A small amount of sugar is added to some Japanese savoury dishes. This might explain why Japanese people don't crave sugary snacks after meals.

japanese horseradish (wasabi)

Most people know this as the green-coloured mustard that is served with sushi. The wasabi root looks like a green ginger root and isn't widely available in the West. You can buy ready-to-use wasabi paste in a tube or in powder form, which needs to be mixed with water.

japanese breadcrumbs (panko)

The biggest difference between panko and standard breadcrumbs is that panko doesn't contain the crust of the bread and the breadcrumbs are bigger. Panko is a better breadcrumb to use for deep-frying, as it absorbs less oil than standard breadcrumbs. It's used for well-known Japanese dishes such as chicken katsu.

japanese seven spice (shichimi togarashi)

This spice mix includes chilli, orange peel, black sesame seeds, white sesame seeds, seaweed, Japanese pepper and ginger. It's often added to Japanese dishes to add a little kick and extra taste. You can buy this ready-made or make your own (see my recipe on page 55).

tofu

Tofu is a soybean product which is low in calories yet high in protein and calcium. The quality and taste of some of the packed tofu available in the West are poor, so make sure to buy good quality GM-free tofu to get a real sense of how great tofu can taste. Fresh tofu can be eaten cold straight from the fridge or added to hot dishes. I find that the Asian speciality stores stock a better selection of good quality tofu.

miso paste

Miso is made from fermented soybeans, salt, rice or barley, and koji (fermentation starter). There are different types of miso, which vary in colour from light brown to dark red/brown. Generally, the lighter the colour the milder the taste. Once miso is opened it should be stored in the refrigerator in an air-tight container. It can be stored in the fridge for about nine months (it will continue to ferment and become more salty over time). It acts as a great marinade for meat, fish or even vegetables.

japanese cooking stock (dashi)

Dashi is used as a base for soups and other Japanese dishes. It's made by soaking kombu (kelp) seaweed, shiitake mushrooms, bonito fish flakes (katsuobushi), or dried fish in water and then bringing to the boil before removing the ingredients. These ingredients fill the stock with umami (the fifth taste).*

instant stock/dashi (dashi no moto)

Instant dashi is a dry ingredient that comes in granules and can be used to replace home-made dashi. The most popular type of instant dashi granules available is called 'hon-dashi', made by a company called Ajinomoto. Using instant dashi in Japanese cooking is similar to using stock cubes for cooking here in the West.

shiitake mushrooms

Both fresh and dried shiitake mushrooms are used widely in Japanese cooking for dishes such as stir-fries and home-made stocks.

bonito fish flakes (katsuobushi)

Katsuobushi is used along with kombu (kelp) seaweed to make Japanese cooking stock (dashi). It also goes well as a topping on different dishes, such as fresh tofu and Japanese-style pancakes (okonomiyaki). Depending on where you live, it can be difficult to get and a little expensive. It's available in most Asian speciality stores.

seaweed (kaiso)

Seaweed is an important part of the Japanese diet, from sushi making to simple stocks and salads. Here is a list of the seaweeds that I regularly use for cooking and that you can find in my recipes throughout this book:

kombu (kelp) seaweed

It's filled with umami (the fifth taste) and one of the main ingredients used to make Japanese cooking stock (dashi). It's also used for salads and stews. Kelp seaweed can be found along the coast of Ireland.

nori seaweed

Nori is best known outside of Japan for wrapping sushi rolls and onigiri (Japanese rice balls). Nori can be bought as roasted seaweed sheets or milled (aonori). This type of seaweed is relatively easy to find in most supermarkets. Once opened, nori sheets need to be stored in an airtight container or they will lose their crispy texture. Ao-nori (milled nori) is often sprinkled over dishes such as okonomiyaki and yakisoba just before serving.

wakame seaweed

Wakame can be bought as small dried pieces. It is added to miso soup and salads. Be careful how much dried wakame you add to a dish as these tiny pieces of seaweed expand once they are in water.

dillisk/dulse seaweed

This is a reddish-brown seaweed that you can easily find along the coast of Ireland. It is packed with vitamins and minerals. It can be used in cooking and baking.

red pickled ginger (beni shoga)

This is a type of Japanese pickle made from thin strips of ginger and flavoured with a type of plum brine called 'umezu', which gives it a bright red colour. It is often used as a topping for dishes such as Japanese curry and yakisoba. It also goes really well with fresh oysters (see my recipe on page 127). This is a little more complicated to make than the pickled ginger mentioned below called 'gari', so people tend to buy it ready-made – it can be found in Asian speciality stores.

pickled ginger (gari)

This is a type of Japanese pickle made from thin slices of ginger flavoured with

sugar and vinegar. It is often served with sushi as it helps to cleanse the palate. You can make this from scratch at home or buy it ready-made in large supermarkets or Asian speciality stores.

sesame seeds (goma)

Sesame seeds are used a lot in Japanese cooking to add extra flavour and nutritional value, such as protein and calcium. They can be sprinkled over dishes before serving but also roasted and ground before adding to sauces.

japanese potato starch (katakuriko) or cornflour

Either of these can be used as a thickening agent for soups or sauces. They can also be used along with spices to coat meat, fish or vegetables before frying.

*author's note

Before living in Japan I had been familiar with the four basic tastes – sweet, sour, salty and bitter. However, while living there I learned about 'umami', the fifth taste. It's probably best described as a savoury taste that isn't salty. Basic ingredients used in Japanese cooking, such as kelp seaweed, bonito fish flakes and shiitake mushrooms, are filled with umami and are the ingredients used to make Japanese stock. Umami can also be found in abundance in Italian cuisine in foods such as tomatoes and Parmesan cheese.

dillisk

milled
nori

milled dillisk

nori sheet

ground kelp

kelp

wakame

notes for the reader

- A measured cup of uncooked rice is equal to 160g.

- All recipes in the book state Japanese white rice in the ingredients. However, if you prefer to use short-grain brown rice please refer to the brown rice cooking instructions on page 33.

- In the recipes throughout the book I use vegetable oil as this is what's traditionally used in Japan for cooking. Please feel free to use your preferred cooking oil for any of my recipes in this book, but remember that for Japanese cooking you should avoid using strong-flavoured oils as they will change the taste of the dish.

- Most recipes and sauces in this book are versatile, so get creative and change the meat and/or vegetables!

- Use your fishmonger and butcher as a source of information. Don't hesitate to ask them to do extra things, such as descaling and filleting fish, deboning chicken legs and thighs, and so on.

- Use free-range or organic eggs and chicken meat if possible.

- Traditionally white sugar is used in Japanese cooking. However, please feel free to use healthier options such as brown sugar or, for some recipes, honey.

RICE

The first thing to learn before you start cooking Japanese food at home is how to cook Japanese rice properly. In this chapter I'll begin by teaching you the steps involved in washing and cooking Japanese rice using either a rice cooker or a saucepan.

To understand the importance of rice in the Japanese diet you only need to look at the word 'gohan', which means both meal and rice. A typical Japanese home-cooked meal always includes a bowl of rice accompanied by soup and several other communal dishes, including vegetables, fish and meat, to give a nutritionally balanced meal.

I lived in a rural village called Nishiyama on the western coast of Japan for two years. It was surrounded by endless rice fields and mountains. There I got to truly experience the importance of rice in Japanese society. I remember one neighbour who warmly welcomed me to Nishiyama village with gifts of his own harvested rice and seasonal vegetables. I became good friends with him and his wife, and learned so much from them about Japanese food and culture. One day they brought me along to their rice field to watch their son plant rice seeds. After witnessing the hard work involved in planting, cultivating and harvesting rice, I gained a deeper appreciation for this sacred grain.

At home I prefer to serve rice in small Japanese-style bowls rather than on plates, as it's easier to control portion sizes this way. The concept of communal eating and the use of chopsticks during eating also help control the amount of food eaten during a Japanese meal, without people having to make a conscious effort to do so.

japanese white rice

Japanese rice is a type of short-grain rice that has to be washed in a particular way to remove the excess starch. To get the perfect bowl of rice follow the steps below. Most Japanese people leave the rice sitting in the sieve for about 15 minutes before cooking. If you don't have time you can skip this step.

You'll need

bowl

rice

water

sieve

1 Place the measured rice in a medium-sized bowl, cover with cold water and gently rub the rice grains against each other using your hands.

2 Drain the rice, add more water and repeat two or three times until the water runs almost clear.

3 Finally place the washed rice in a sieve to drain excess water.

how to cook Japanese white rice

using a rice cooker

If you have a rice cooker at home, please wash the rice as instructed above and then follow the manufacturer's instructions to cook the rice. Generally the rice cooker will include a rice measuring cup and a measure on the inside of the rice cooker bowl to guide you on the amount of water to add.

using a saucepan (amount given serves 4 people)

You'll need

heavy-based saucepan with a tight lid

2 cups Japanese rice (using a measured rice cup this weighs 320g), uncooked

2½ cups cold water

1 Transfer the washed rice to the saucepan.

2 Add two and a half cups of cold water, cover and slowly bring to the boil over a medium to high heat (this takes about 10 minutes depending on the size of the saucepan and heat source).

3 Once the water is boiling, reduce to a medium to low heat and continue to cook, covered, for a further 6 minutes or until the water is fully absorbed into the rice.

4 Without lifting the lid (if possible – if the lid on the saucepan is not clear you may want to slightly lift it to check if the water is fully absorbed), remove from the heat and set aside for another 10 minutes to allow the rice to continue cooking in its own steam.

5 Use a rice spatula to gently fold the rice, then serve.

short-grain brown rice

In some parts of Japan brown rice is eaten, but in most cases Japanese people eat white rice. Recently, people are returning to whole foods and replacing white rice with brown rice due to the loss of vitamins and fibre in polished white rice. Brown rice only needs to be washed in cold water once compared to white rice, which is washed in cold water a few times to remove excess starch. Keep in mind that it takes longer to cook brown rice.

how to cook brown rice

using a rice cooker

I have a Japanese rice cooker at home that my friend got for me while visiting Asia. Japanese rice cookers tend to have lots of functions, including a special function for cooking brown rice. If your rice cooker doesn't have this then it's likely that it won't cook brown rice properly, leaving it slightly undercooked and hard to chew. In this case you should try cooking brown rice in a saucepan as instructed below. If you'd like to buy a Japanese rice cooker you can purchase one online or in an Asian speciality store.

using a saucepan (amount given serves 4 people)

You'll need

heavy-based saucepan with a tight lid

2 cups short-grain brown rice (using a measured rice cup this weighs 320g), uncooked

3 cups cold water

1   Wash the brown rice with cold water and drain.

2   Transfer the washed rice to the saucepan.

3   Add three cups of cold water. Now leave the rice to soak for at least 1 hour, or up to a few hours if possible (this will help the rice to cook faster).

4   When the rice is finished soaking, cover and slowly bring to the boil over a medium to high heat (this takes about 10 minutes depending on the size of the saucepan and heat source).

5   Once the water is boiling, reduce to a medium to low heat and continue to cook, covered, for another 30 minutes, or until the water is fully absorbed into the rice (the cooking time will depend on how long the rice was soaking).

6   Without lifting the lid (if possible), remove from the heat and set aside for another 10 minutes to cook in its own steam.

7   Use a rice spatula to gently mix the rice, then serve.

onigiri
rice balls

Onigiri is Japan's version of a sandwich. These rice balls are one of Japan's most loved convenient foods and come in different shapes, including triangular and oval. They are mainly enjoyed as a lunch box filler and can be bought ready-made in Japanese convenience stores and supermarkets.

What follows are my three favourite onigiri recipes, which I use for picnics, family day trips and, of course, lunch box fillers. I found the tuna mayo onigiri in a Japanese convenience store when I was a student in Japan and couldn't believe that they only cost about €1. I missed them so much when I returned to Ireland that I started making my own!

home-made furikake
dried seasoning

I remember large sections of Japanese supermarkets dedicated to different types of ready-made furikake. Outside Japan you can buy it in Asian speciality stores, but this simple recipe can be made in minutes at home. This recipe works really well for onigiri, to add colour and flavour. I also sprinkle it over a plain bowl of steamed rice, a salad or cooked fish (the options are endless!).

My little boy Scott calls this dried seasoning 'magic sprinkles' and, funnily enough, from a nutritional perspective these sprinkles really are magic. One of the main ingredients in this recipe is dillisk (also called dulse) seaweed, which is high in iron, calcium, protein and fibre. It is also a natural source of essential vitamins, ions and sea salt.

8 tablespoons raw white sesame seeds

8 tablespoons raw black sesame seeds

8 tablespoons milled dillisk

1   Toast the sesame seeds in a non-stick pan on a medium heat until they start to pop. Be careful not to burn them as this takes only a few minutes. Set aside to cool.

2   Put the milled dillisk along with the cooled mixed roasted sesame seeds in a bowl and mix well.

3   Store in an airtight container. These will keep for a month or so.

onigiri with furikake

1   Leave the piping-hot cooked rice aside for a minute or so to avoid burning your hands.

2   Dip your hands into the bowl of water, then sprinkle salt on the palms of your hands.

3   Take a handful of rice and, using both hands, shape it into a triangular or oval shape pressing firmly on it so it's secure and won't fall apart (see picture d on page 39).

4   Take one of the strips of nori and wrap around the bottom of the rice ball (see picture e on page 39).

5   Sprinkle furikake over the top of the rice or place furikake on a flat plate and roll the rice ball over it if you prefer to completely coat the rice ball in furikake. In this case there's no need to put the nori strip on the rice ball.

6   Continue to make the rice balls until all the rice is used.

Makes 6–8 onigiri

cooked Japanese white rice (2 rice cooker-measured cups of uncooked rice, 320g)

bowl of cold water, for dampening your hands to make the rice balls

salt (preferably freshly ground sea salt)

1 sheet of nori – (make 8 strips by folding it in half, then a quarter, then one-eighth and then tear it with your hands or alternatively cut into 8 pieces using kitchen scissors or a sharp knife)

a few tablespoons of furikake (for the home-made furikake recipe see opposite)

✳ Tip

Remember to make the rice balls smaller for younger kids.

onigiri with tuna mayo filling

Makes 6–8 onigiri

160g tin of tuna in brine, drained

1 tablespoon mayonnaise

1 teaspoon wasabi

cooked Japanese white rice (2 rice cooker-measured cups of uncooked rice, 320g)

bowl of cold water, for dampening your hands to make the rice balls

salt (preferably freshly ground sea salt)

1 sheet of nori – (make 8 strips by folding it in half, then a quarter, then one-eighth and then tear it with your hands or alternatively cut into 8 pieces using kitchen scissors or a sharp knife)

a few tablespoons of sesame seeds

1   Mix the tuna, mayonnaise and wasabi together in a bowl and set aside.

2   Leave the piping hot cooked rice aside for a minute or so to avoid burning your hands.

3   Dip your hands into the bowl of water and sprinkle salt on the palms of your hands.

4   Take a handful of rice and, using both hands, shape it into an oval shape. Then, using your thumb, make a hollow in the middle of the rice ball, deep enough to fit one tablespoon of the tuna mayo (see a).

5   Place the tuna mayo in the hollow. Gently fold the walls of the rice ball over the filling until it is completely covered (see b–c).

6   Using both hands shape the rice ball into a triangular or oval shape, pressing firmly on the rice so it's secure and won't fall apart (see d).

7   Take one of the strips of nori and wrap around the bottom of the rice ball. Sprinkle sesame seeds over the top (see e–f).

8   Continue to make the rice balls until all the rice is used.

✳   Tip

To keep onigiri fresh wrap them individually in cling film or tinfoil.

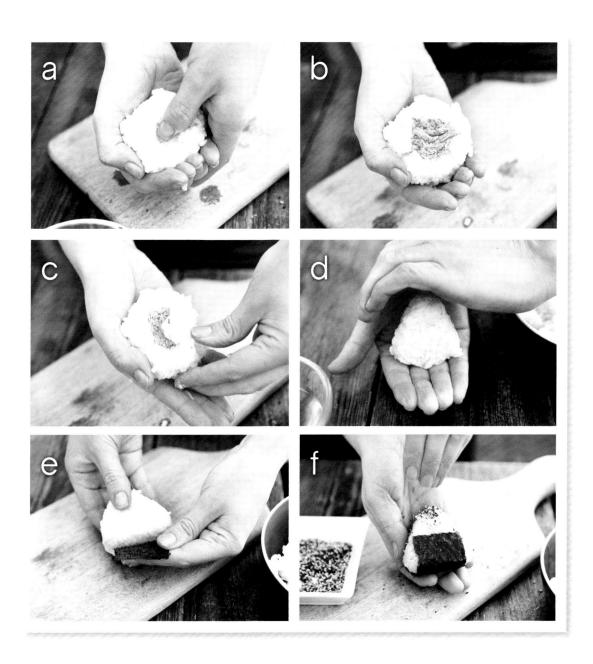

onigiri mixed with chicken & spring onion

Makes 8–10 onigiri

vegetable oil

1 medium carrot (100g), cut into very small cubes

1 chicken breast, cut into very small cubes

1 teaspoon sake

1 teaspoon soy sauce

pepper to season

1 tablespoon freshly grated ginger

cooked Japanese white rice (1 rice cooker-measured cup of uncooked rice, 160g)

1 spring onion, finely diced

bowl of cold water, for dampening your hands to make the rice balls

1   Heat some vegetable oil on a medium heat in a non-stick frying pan.

2   Toss in the carrot and cook for a few minutes, then add the chicken pieces, sake, soy sauce and pepper. Mix well together.

3   Continue to cook for about 5 minutes or until the chicken is cooked through (take one piece of chicken and cut down the middle to see if it's cooked through – it should be white).

4   Finally add the ginger and cook for 2 minutes. Then take off the heat and place on kitchen paper to absorb the excess oil (too much oil will prevent the rice balls from sticking).

5   Transfer the hot cooked rice to a large bowl. Add the chicken mix and diced spring onion. Mix well together.

6   Dip your hands into the bowl of water and take a handful of the rice mix. Using both hands, shape the rice ball into a triangular or oval shape, pressing firmly on the rice so it's secure and won't fall apart.

7   Continue to make the rice balls until all the rice mix is used.

*   Tip

If you're making the chicken onigiri for kids, replace the spring onion with either fresh or defrosted green peas.

chicken & pak choi fried rice

1   Heat some vegetable oil in a non-stick frying pan on a medium heat.

2   Add the garlic and ginger and fry for a minute or so.

3   Add in the chicken pieces, pour the sake over the chicken and continue to fry until the chicken is cooked through.

4   Add the pak choi stalks only and mix.

5   Push the ingredients to one side of the frying pan making room for the egg. Pour the beaten egg into the cleared part of the frying pan and fry for a minute or so (try not to overcook the egg at this stage).

6   Add the pak choi green leaf ends and the cooked rice. Mix all the ingredients together.

7   Drizzle with soy sauce and sesame oil just before taking off the heat. Mix well and serve.

Serves 2

vegetable oil

1 clove of garlic, peeled and thinly sliced

1 tablespoon freshly grated ginger

1 chicken breast, cut into bite-size pieces

1 tablespoon sake

large handful of pak choi leaves, washed and roughly chopped

1 egg, beaten

cooked Japanese white rice (1 rice cooker-measured cup of uncooked rice, 160g)

2 tablespoons soy sauce

sesame oil to season

seasoned boiled rice

This recipe is an easy way to incorporate your favourite vegetables into boiled rice. The kelp and shiitake mushrooms add umami and a depth of flavour to the dish.

1   Prepare and cook the rice as outlined on page 32 adding the sake, kombu, shiitake mushrooms and carrot pieces to the water before starting to cook the rice. This can be done in a rice cooker or saucepan.

2   When the rice is cooked, cover it and set aside for 10 minutes to cook in its own steam. Remove the kombu, then toss in the handful of peas. Use a rice spatula to mix all the ingredients evenly together.

3   Serve on its own or with a fish or meat dish.

Serves 4

2 cups Japanese white rice (320g)

1 tablespoon sake

1 strip of dried kombu (kelp)

a few handfuls of shiitake mushroom, roughly chopped

1 small carrot, peeled and cut into small cubes

handful of frozen peas, blanched in a cup of boiling water

garlic fried rice
(topped with a fried egg)

This is one of the most viewed recipes on my blog. I think this is because it's so easy to make and uses very few ingredients.

Serves 2

vegetable oil

4 cloves of garlic, peeled and thinly sliced

cooked Japanese white rice (1 rice cooker-measured cup of uncooked rice, 160g)

soy sauce to season

sesame oil to season

2 eggs

shichimi togarashi (Japanese seven spice) to serve

1   In a non-stick frying pan heat a generous amount of vegetable oil over a medium to high heat and add the garlic.

2   Fry the garlic until slightly browned and crispy, then remove from the pan, place on a small plate and set aside.

3   Add the cooked rice to the garlic-infused oil still sitting in the base of the frying pan and fry until the rice is evenly covered in the oil and hot. Add the garlic.

4   Drizzle a small amount of soy sauce and sesame oil over the rice and mix well. Take off the heat and divide between two plates.

5   Using the same frying pan, add more oil if necessary and put over a medium to high heat.

6   Crack the eggs into the frying pan and cook to your liking (preferably leave the egg yolk runny).

7   Place one fried egg on each plate on top of the rice.

8   Sprinkle shichimi togarashi over the egg and rice to serve.

SOUPS & SALADS

This chapter introduces the basic steps to making your own Japanese cooking stock and soup at home. This might sound like a lot of effort, but Japanese stocks and soups actually take less time to make than those with which we are familiar here in the West.

I've dedicated a large part of this chapter to one of Japan's most loved comfort foods – miso soup. Traditionally miso soup is served with every Japanese meal, including breakfast, alongside rice and other communal dishes. I'd love to see you integrate miso soup into your lifestyle in a non-traditional way if this works better for you. One of my miso soup recipes works perfectly on its own for breakfast or brunch. Some of my other recipes can be enjoyed as a light lunch or dinner along with one of my onigiri 'rice ball' recipes from the previous chapter.

When I worked in Japan I had a bento box with an integrated compartment for miso soup, so I was able to easily pack miso soup with my lunch every day. Now that I'm living in Ireland I find my tea flask works perfectly to store my miso soup for work lunches.

You'll notice throughout this book that in Japanese cooking most dishes are reduced to a simmer after they come to the boil. This allows dishes to cook slowly, thus maximising the flavour and minimising the loss of nutrients. This also applies to miso soup, so once miso paste is added to the dashi (stock) it should only be simmered.

In the last part of this chapter I share some of my favourite fusion salad recipes with you. They are not traditional Japanese recipes, but I've used Japanese ingredients to create really light and tasty salad dressings in order to make an ordinary salad more interesting.

dashi

japanese cooking stock

Dashi is a type of cooking stock used as a base for soups and other dishes in Japanese cuisine. It is surprisingly easy to make compared to stocks here in the West. The secret to a good Japanese stock is to use ingredients filled with umami – 'the fifth taste'. Traditionally, dried fish flakes called 'katsuobushi' and kelp seaweed are the basis for Japanese stock. Since katsuobushi is quite difficult to get outside Japan and expensive to buy, I tend to use kelp seaweed only or a mix of kelp seaweed and shiitake mushrooms, as these raw ingredients are also filled with umami and are widely available. We have an abundance of kelp seaweed here in Ireland, which can be bought in health stores, large supermarkets and fishmongers, so Ireland really is the ideal place to make dashi!

dashi no moto: instant stock

Instant stock (also called instant dashi) is a dry ingredient that comes in granules and can be used to replace home-made dashi. Using instant dashi in Japanese cooking is similar to using stock cubes for cooking here in the West. Outside Japan it can be difficult to source so, depending on where you live, it may be easier to make home-made dashi. The most popular type of instant dashi granules available is called 'hon-dashi', made by a company called Ajinomoto.

To use instant dashi granules for any of the miso soup recipes on pages 60–62 add 1 teaspoon of instant dashi granules to 1 litre of water.

I recommend making dashi from scratch if possible, as nothing compares to the depth of flavour in home-made dashi and you also have the comfort of knowing exactly what's in the stock. What follows are three recipes for home-made dashi.

kombu dashi
kelp stock

Makes 1 litre

1 litre water

40g dried kombu (kelp) –
equivalent to two postcard-
sized pieces

1   Put 1 litre of cold water into a large saucepan.

2   Add the kombu to the water and leave to soak for at
     least 30 minutes. If you have time leave to soak for
     a few hours or overnight (in this case, place it in the
     fridge). This will fill the water with the goodness and
     umami from the seaweed.

3   Heat the water until it comes to the boil and then
     remove the kombu immediately.

4   This can be stored in the fridge for about 3 days, or
     you can freeze it.

kombu & katsuobushi dashi
kelp & dried fish-flakes stock

For this stock it's possible to make two batches to get the most out of the ingredients. The first batch is called 'ichiban dashi' and the second batch is called 'niban dashi'. The second batch is weaker than the first batch since it's re-using the ingredients used to make the first batch.

ichiban dashi: 'first stock'

1   Put 1 litre of cold water into a large saucepan.

2   Add the kombu to the water and leave it to soak for about 20–30 minutes (or longer if you have time).

3   Heat the water until it comes to the boil and remove the kombu immediately.

4   Add the katsuobushi to the water and bring to the boil again. Once the water starts to boil take it off the heat and let it sit until the katsuobushi sinks to the bottom of the saucepan.

5   Drain the dashi through a sieve lined with kitchen paper.

6   This stock can be stored in the fridge for about 3 days, or you can freeze it.

niban dashi: 'second stock'

As I explained above, you can make a weaker stock called *niban dashi* with the used kombu and katsuobushi from the first batch of stock. Simply put 1 litre of water in a large saucepan and add the used katsuobushi and kombu to the water. Slowly bring the water to a boil and then immediately reduce to a simmer. Remove the kombu and leave simmering for a few more minutes. Take off the heat and set aside for a few minutes. Then drain using a sieve lined with kitchen paper.

Makes 1 litre

1 litre water

20g dried kombu (kelp) – a piece about the size of a postcard

20g katsuobushi (dried bonito flakes)

kombu & shiitake dashi
kelp & shiitake stock

Makes 1 litre

1 litre water

20g dried kombu (kelp)
– a piece about the size of a
postcard

3 dried shiitake mushrooms

1   Put 1 litre of cold water in a large saucepan.

2   Add the kombu and shiitake mushrooms to the water
    and leave to soak for at least 30 minutes. If you
    have time leave to soak for a few hours or overnight
    (in this case, place in the fridge). This will fill the
    water with the goodness and umami from both the
    seaweed and the mushrooms.

3   Heat the water until it comes to the boil and then
    remove the kombu and mushrooms immediately.

4   This can be stored in the fridge for about 3 days, or
    you can freeze it.

✳   Tip

    This is an ideal dashi for vegetarians.

shichimi togarashi

japanese seven spice

This wonderful collection of seven spices adds an interesting dimension to the taste of a dish and also adds a nutritional explosion, with each spice boasting different health benefits. In summary, these seven spices possess strong anti-cancerous and anti-inflammatory properties; contain high levels of fibre, iron, calcium and protein; help to lower cholesterol; and aid digestion.

At home I sprinkle this over soups, stews and noodle dishes once they are ready to be eaten. It also works really well as a seasoning for meat, fish or seafood.

1   Place the orange zest on a baking tray in a preheated fan oven at 100°C for about 20 minutes or until it's completely dried (keep a close eye on this as it can burn easily). Remove from the oven and set aside to cool.

2   Using a pestle and mortar, grind the orange zest into a powder, then transfer to a bowl along with all the other ingredients and mix well.

3   Store in an airtight container for a month or so.

zest of 1 large orange, preferably organic

1 tablespoon cayenne pepper

½ tablespoon ground Japanese sansho pepper or Chinese sichuan pepper

1 tablespoon black sesame seeds, roasted

1 tablespoon white sesame seeds, roasted

½ tablespoon ground ginger

1 tablespoon milled nori (or substitute with milled Irish dillisk)

miso soup

Two of the main ingredients used to make miso soup are dashi (Japanese cooking stock) and miso. Miso is a fermented paste made from soybeans, rice or barley, salt and koji (a fermentation starter). It's known for its undeniable health benefits, including anti-cancerous properties and aiding digestion. It's also a rich source of protein and vitamin B12.

There are three main types of miso paste – white (shiro miso), yellow (shinshu miso) and red (aka miso). Each miso paste has unique characteristics, but in general the darker the miso colour the stronger the taste, so if you haven't tried miso before it might be better to start with white miso paste.

In recent years miso paste has become widely available outside Japan in large supermarkets, Asian speciality stores and health shops. There's also a wider range to choose from, including organic miso pastes made with brown rice (genmai miso) and barley (mugi miso).

Once miso is opened it should be stored in the refrigerator in an airtight container and will last for about 9 months.

You can use any of the stock recipes on pages 52–54 to make my three miso soup recipes following. Feel free to be creative and add your own favourite ingredients.

To consume miso soup the Japanese way, hold the bowl to your mouth to drink the soup and use chopsticks to eat the bite-size ingredients.

cabbage & shichimi togarashi (japanese seven spice) miso soup

Serves 4

1 litre dashi (see pages 52–54 for dashi recipes)

a few handfuls of savoy cabbage leaves (about 200g), washed and roughly chopped

2–3 tablespoons miso paste, depending on your own taste

shichimi togarashi to season

1 Heat the dashi in a large saucepan.

2 Once the dashi is boiling add the cabbage leaves and cook for 10 minutes.

3 Dilute the miso paste in a small cup of dashi taken from the saucepan.

4 Reduce the soup to a very low heat and add the miso paste to the saucepan. Gently stir into the soup until mixed through.

5 Serve in a bowl and season with shichimi togarashi.

wakame & tofu miso soup
with poached egg

This recipe is ideal for breakfast or brunch and will give you a great start to the day. Japanese people consider breakfast to be one of the most important meals of the day. A traditional Japanese breakfast includes a bowl of rice, miso soup and side dishes which are usually left over from the previous day's dinner. It's not always practical to prepare a full traditional Japanese breakfast, but this hearty miso soup is a nice compromise.

1   Heat the dashi in a large saucepan.

2   Once the dashi is boiling add the wakame seaweed and reduce the heat so that the dashi is simmering.

3   Gently toss the tofu pieces into the saucepan.

4   Dilute the miso paste in a small cup of dashi taken from the saucepan, then add to the saucepan and gently stir into the soup until mixed through.

5   To serve, pour the miso soup into a bowl. Place a poached egg on top of it and garnish with spring onion and shichimi togarashi.

Serves 4

1 litre dashi (see pages 52–54 for dashi recipes)

1 tablespoon dried wakame seaweed

300g tofu (preferably GM free), cut into bite-size cubes

2–3 tablespoons miso paste, depending on your own taste

1 poached egg per each bowl serving

spring onion, finely diced, to garnish

shichimi togarashi to season

clam miso soup

This is a simple recipe where the ingredients will speak for themselves. Make sure to source the clams from a reliable fishmonger so they are as fresh as possible.

Serves 4

300g fresh clams

1 litre dashi (see pages 52–54 for dashi recipes)

2 tablespoons miso paste

2 handfuls of baby spinach, roughly chopped to garnish

1   Clean the clams thoroughly. If any of the clams are open tap them on a hard surface and if they do not close then discard them.

2   In a large saucepan bring the dashi to the boil.

3   Add the clams and boil for a few minutes until they open (discard any closed ones), then reduce to a simmer.

4   Dilute the miso paste in a small cup of dashi taken from the saucepan, then add to the saucepan and gently stir into the soup until mixed through.

5   Place the baby spinach in the bottom of the serving bowls and pour the miso soup and clams on top of it.

egg-drop soup

This is a very delicate and mild soup that goes really well with dishes such as gyoza (see page 83) and fried rice (see pages 41 and 46).

1 Bring 1 litre of kombu and shiitake dashi to the boil.

2 Reduce to a simmer and add the soy sauce and mirin.

3 Dilute the cornflour in a small amount of water and add to the soup. Season with salt and pepper and gently stir.

4 Carefully add the beaten egg by slowly pouring it around the outer edges of the saucepan into the dashi, moving in a circular motion (ideally use a jug to pour the beaten egg into the saucepan).

5 Use the shiitake mushrooms left over from making the stock, finely chop them and add them to the soup.

6 Serve in a bowl, lightly season with sesame oil and top with chopped parsley.

Serves 4

1 litre dashi (see kombu and shiitake dashi recipe on page 54)

2 tablespoons soy sauce

1 tablespoon mirin

1 tablespoon cornflour or potato starch

salt and pepper to season

2 eggs, beaten

dried shiitake mushrooms left over from the stock

sesame oil to season

flat-leaf parsley, chopped

Rice
Vinegar

fusion salads

In Japan, salads tend to be served on the side rather than as a main meal which is common here in the West, especially during the summer months. Mine can be used for either. My salad dressings are inspired by Japanese ingredients such as soy sauce and rice vinegar. They are light yet full of flavour. I hope you enjoy them.

These recipes serve one person as a main course or two people as a starter or side.

roast sweet potato &
baby spinach salad

1 Place the sweet potato cubes in a roasting tin and coat with a mix of vegetable oil and sesame oil. Cook for about 20 minutes in a preheated fan oven at 170°C or until cooked through, then allow to cool.

2 Pour all the ingredients for the salad dressing into an empty jam jar, put the lid on and shake well until the sugar is dissolved.

3 Toss the baby spinach, avocado and tomato into a salad bowl.

4 Add the sweet potato.

5 Just before serving pour the salad dressing over the salad and mix well using your hands.

Serves 1–2

100g sweet potato, peeled and cut into small cubes

vegetable oil

sesame oil

100g baby spinach, washed

1 ripened avocado, cut into bite-size pieces

1 tomato, cut into bite-size pieces

For the dressing

1 teaspoon soy sauce

1 teaspoon orange zest, preferably from an organic orange

2 tablespoons orange juice

1 teaspoon lemon juice

½ teaspoon brown sugar

1 tablespoon olive oil

irish goat's cheese, fig & apple salad

In Ireland we have fantastic cheese producers who make excellent quality cheese. The fig, apple and walnuts in this recipe offer diverse flavours and textures when matched with the soft goat's cheese and refreshing rice vinegar dressing. This is a favourite in my house during the summer months.

Serves 1–2 people

100g mixed salad leaves

1 fresh fig, cut into bite-size pieces (if fresh figs are not available use dried fig or add more apple instead)

½ pink lady apple, cut into matchsticks

80g soft goat's cheese, rolled into small balls using a teaspoon

handful of chopped walnuts to serve

For the dressing

3 tablespoons rice vinegar

1 tablespoon olive oil

2 teaspoons brown sugar

1   Pour all the ingredients for the salad dressing into an empty jam jar, put the lid on and shake well until the sugar is dissolved.

2   Toss all the salad ingredients (except the walnuts) into a salad bowl.

3   Just before serving pour the salad dressing over the salad and mix well using your hands.

4   Place a handful of walnuts on top.

seared tuna & mango salad

When making this recipe make sure to lightly sear the tuna as I truly believe tuna tastes better either raw or lightly seared. Once tuna is cooked it becomes tough and loses its flavour. This salad is particularly nice eaten while the tuna is warm, so don't waste any time once it's ready and try to eat it straight away.

1   Mix together the sesame seeds, salt and pepper on a flat plate.

2   Place the tuna on the plate and coat each side in sesame seeds.

3   Heat a little vegetable oil in a non-stick frying pan on a medium to high heat.

4   Place the tuna on the pan and sear each side lightly (less than 1 minute for each side).

5   Transfer to a chopping board and, using a sharp knife, thinly slice the tuna.

6   Place the mixed salad leaves on a serving dish along with the mango strips.

7   Carefully place the tuna slices on top.

8   Mix all the ingredients for the dressing in a bowl and, just before serving, pour over the salad.

Serves 1–2

mixed sesame seeds to coat the tuna

salt and pepper to season the tuna

100g fresh tuna steak/loin

vegetable oil

a few handfuls of mixed salad leaves

1 ripened mango, peeled and cut into strips

For the dressing

2 teaspoons soy sauce

1 teaspoon rice vinegar

½ teaspoon sesame oil

CHICKEN

In most Asian countries, including Japan, dark chicken meat (i.e. chicken legs and thighs) is in high demand compared to white chicken meat (i.e. breast). In fact, Japanese people consider chicken breast to have little flavour or nutritional value in comparison. In Ireland dark chicken meat is priced very reasonably compared to chicken breasts, so it makes economic sense to add it to your shopping list! For some of the chicken dishes in this chapter I use the leg and thigh with the bones and skin removed. If you'd prefer not to do this at home, any good butcher will have no problem doing this for you.

'Yakitori-ya' is a type of Japanese restaurant which specialises in grilled chicken. I loved going to these restaurants when I lived in Japan, as the dining setting is quite casual, with a bustling atmosphere and amazing food. They usually serve a wide variety of chicken parts on skewers, which are grilled over charcoal. Then the meat is flavoured with either salt – 'shio' – or a sauce called 'tare'. Be careful what you order though, as you could end up eating popular chicken delicacies like chicken heart, skin and even cartilage if you can't read the menu properly!

In this chapter I've included traditional Japanese recipes, such as 'oyako-don', and modern recipes that I created using Japanese ingredients, such as miso roast chicken. I've also included some all-time favourites both in Japan and abroad, such as chicken katsu curry, gyoza and teriyaki chicken wings.

oyako-don
chicken & egg rice bowl

Oyako-don literally translates as 'parent and child rice bowl'. The chicken represents the 'parent' and the egg represents the 'child'. The term 'don' means bowl and is added to the end of dishes that are served on a bowl of rice. After eating this dish in a Japanese restaurant, I had to learn how to make it at home so I could have it whenever I wanted it! I love the sweet and savoury flavour of the broth and the way the beaten egg is slightly steam-cooked over the tender chicken pieces. It's now one of my family's favourite dishes.

Serves 2

200g chicken leg and/or thigh meat (skin and bone removed), cut into bite-size pieces

1 medium onion, peeled and thinly sliced

2 eggs, beaten

2 bowls of boiled rice to serve

spring onion to garnish

For the broth

100ml chicken stock (for home-made chicken stock see page 154)

1 teaspoon sugar

2 tablespoons sake

2 tablespoons soy sauce

1 tablespoon mirin

1   Put all the ingredients for the broth in a small non-stick frying pan or saucepan and mix well together.

2   Toss the chicken pieces and onion into the broth and place on a high heat until it comes to the boil. Then reduce to a simmer and continue to cook for about 10 minutes or until the chicken is cooked through.

3   Carefully pour the beaten egg evenly over the chicken and onion sitting in the broth.

4   Cover the pan with a lid and continue simmering until the egg is nearly cooked.

5   Place equal amounts over two bowls of hot boiled rice, pouring any excess liquid over the dish.

6   Garnish with finely sliced spring onion.

✳ Tip

Try not to overcook the egg. Remember that it will continue to cook in its own heat and also when placed on the hot rice.

roast miso chicken

This is a simple way to add an interesting twist to your typical roast chicken. The miso marinade tenderises and adds a really nice flavour to the chicken meat.

Serves 4

1½kg whole chicken

For the marinade

3 tablespoons miso paste

1½ tablespoons mirin

1 tablespoon sesame oil

2 tablespoons vegetable oil

1 teaspoon shichimi togarashi

4 tablespoons water

For roasting

tinfoil

3 tablespoons cold water

1   Put all the ingredients for the marinade in a bowl and mix well together. Using your hands rub into the whole chicken (and also between the skin and chicken breast if you like). Leave on the chicken before roasting for at least 30 minutes. If you have time you can leave for a few hours or overnight, in the fridge.

2   Preheat a fan oven to 180°C.

3   Transfer the chicken to a roasting tin lined with tinfoil and pour the water into the base of the roasting tin. Completely cover the chicken with the tinfoil.

4   Cook in the oven for about 2 hours, or until the chicken is cooked through.

5   Once the chicken is cooked, leave to rest for 10 minutes before slicing and serving.

chicken karaage
japanese fried chicken

There are lots of festivals (known as matsuri) celebrated in Japan throughout the year and at every festival you'll find popular Japanese street food, including yakisoba (fried noodles), okonomiyaki (Japanese-style pancake) and chicken karaage (Japanese fried chicken). When we lived in Japan my husband and I loved going to these festivals to sample the vast range of street food and soak up the atmosphere.

1   Mix the sake, soy sauce and grated ginger in a medium-sized bowl.

2   Put the chicken pieces in the marinade and stir to make sure they are evenly covered. Set aside for about 10 minutes.

3   Drain the marinade from the chicken pieces and pat with kitchen paper to remove the excess marinade.

4   Generously coat the chicken pieces in cornflour, shaking off any excess.

5   Heat the oil to 170°C. To check the oil temperature drop a bit of cornflour into the saucepan. If it rises to the top of the oil and sizzles, then the oil is hot enough.

6   Carefully place the chicken pieces in the oil and fry for about 5 minutes until the chicken is a golden brown colour and cooked through. Be careful not to overcrowd the pan. If you notice that the chicken pieces are starting to brown too quickly, then the oil is too hot.

7   Arrange the chicken pieces on kitchen paper to absorb any excess oil.

8   Serve with lemon wedges.

Serves 2

4 chicken legs/thighs (skin and bone removed), cut into bite-size pieces

cornflour to coat

vegetable oil for deep-frying

lemon wedges to serve

For the marinade

2 tablespoons sake

2 tablespoons soy sauce

1 tablespoon grated ginger

✳ Tip

To really infuse the flavour, you can leave the chicken pieces in the marinade for a few hours or overnight in the fridge if you have time.

chicken gyoza
chicken dumplings

Gyoza originated in China and is a popular side dish in ramen shops and tapas-style restaurants called 'izakaya'. It is served with a dipping sauce made of equal amounts of soy sauce and rice vinegar with a few drops of sesame chilli oil. You can make these dumplings using different fillings such as minced pork, prawns or vegetables only. I usually make a large batch and freeze them as they cook well from frozen. Remember to steam cook the dumplings for longer if you're cooking them from frozen.

Makes 25–30 gyoza (dumplings)

25–30 gyoza skins

bowl of water for sealing the dumplings

vegetable oil

80ml cold water for steaming

sesame oil to season

For the filling

200g good-quality minced chicken breast

100g cabbage, finely diced

1 spring onion, finely diced

1 tablespoon freshly grated ginger

2 cloves of garlic, peeled and grated

3 shiitake mushrooms, finely chopped

1 tablespoon soy sauce

1 tablespoon sake

1 teaspoon sesame oil

salt and pepper to season

2 tablespoons potato starch

Dipping sauce

2 tablespoons soy sauce

2 tablespoons rice vinegar

a few drops of la-yu (chilli-infused sesame oil) to taste

how to make the dumplings

1   Mix together all the ingredients for the gyoza filling in a large bowl and set aside.

2   Before you start making the dumplings, place the gyoza skins, a clean bowl of water, a teaspoon and a large serving dish on the countertop.

3   Place a gyoza skin on the palm of your hand, take a heaped teaspoon of the filling and place it in the centre of the gyoza skin (see a–b).

4   Moisten the edge of the upper half of the gyoza skin by dipping your finger in the bowl of water and sliding it along the edge (see c).

5   Fold the bottom half of the gyoza skin over the filling so that it meets the moistened upper half (see d).

6   Start to pleat by folding the edges (make one pleat in the middle and two pleats at either side) (see e).

7   Press firmly on all pleats to ensure that the ingredients are secure within the gyoza skin (see f).

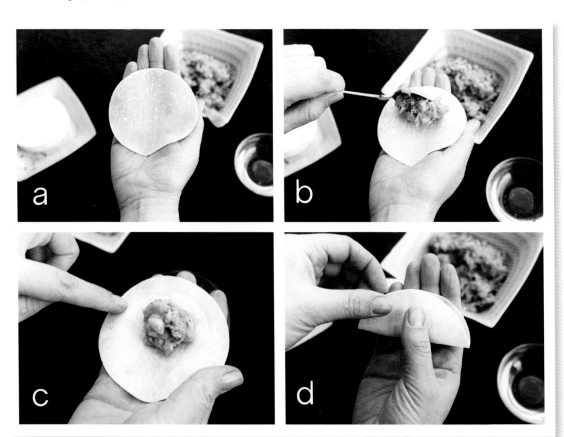

how to cook the dumplings

1   Heat the oil in a non-stick frying pan over a medium to high heat.

2   Place the gyoza in the pan and fry until the base is slightly golden.

3   Pour 80ml of cold water around the edges of the pan and cover with a lid. Leave steaming for 10 minutes or until almost all of the water has evaporated.

4   Remove the lid and continue to fry until the water is fully absorbed.

5   Finally, drizzle the sesame oil over the gyoza and fry until the base of the gyoza is golden brown. Transfer to a serving dish.

6   Mix all the ingredients for the dipping sauce in a small bowl and serve with the gyoza.

negima yakitori
chicken & spring onion skewers

These chicken skewers taste much nicer if you use dark chicken meat. They can be cooked on a grill but also go really well on a barbeque during the summer months.

Makes 8 skewers

4 chicken thighs (skin and bone removed), cut into bite-size/2-inch cubes

3 spring onions, cut into 2-inch pieces

8 wooden skewers, soaked in water for 20 minutes

sesame seeds to garnish

spring onion to garnish

For the sauce

6 tablespoons sake

4 tablespoons mirin

4 tablespoons soy sauce

1 tablespoon sugar

1   Put all the ingredients for the sauce into a saucepan and slowly bring to the boil over a medium heat. Reduce to a simmer on a medium to low heat for 12 minutes or until the sauce starts to thicken (don't reduce it too much or it will caramelise). Transfer to a bowl and set aside.

2   Thread the chicken and spring onion alternatively onto the skewers.

3   Preheat the grill to a high heat.

4   Brush all the skewers with the sauce before putting them under the grill.

5   Place the skewers high in the grill to give a barbeque effect to the chicken.

6   Grill them for about 15 minutes, turning and brushing them with the sauce two or three times during cooking.

7   Garnish with sesame seeds and chopped spring onion.

fiona's home-made japanese curry roux

Japanese curries are much milder and sweeter than Indian curries. A spicy Japanese curry is likely to be the same as a mild Indian curry. Japanese people love curry and you can find speciality curry restaurants dotted throughout the country. Also in the supermarkets you'll find shelves and shelves of ready-made curry roux, the most popular brand being S&B. Although Japanese people tend to buy ready-made curry roux for cooking at home, I'm including my home-made curry roux, partly because it's not as easy to find ready-made packets outside Japan, but most importantly because it's actually really easy to make your own! If you'd like to make this curry spicier, add more cayenne pepper. The measurements below make enough for a batch of sauce to serve 2–4 people, depending on how thick or thin you make it and if it's just to pour over a dish or the main sauce in a dish.

1   Melt the butter on a low heat in a saucepan, then add all the ingredients except the flour and mix well. Continue to cook on a low heat for 10 minutes to bring out the flavours of the spices.

2   Add the flour and mix well to make the curry roux. Take off the heat and let cool.

Serves 2–4

2 tablespoons butter

2 tablespoons pure apple juice

1 tablespoon vegetable oil

2 teaspoons garam masala

4 teaspoons curry powder

2 teaspoons soy sauce

2 teaspoons Worcestershire sauce

2 teaspoons tomato ketchup

¼ teaspoon cayenne pepper (optional, to add spice)

3 tablespoons plain flour

✳ Notes

To make a curry sauce, add the curry roux and about 300ml of water to a saucepan and let it simmer until it thickens to the consistency you prefer.

If you are vegetarian, remove the Worcestershire sauce.

✳ Tip

Remove the cayenne pepper to make it more suitable for kids.

chicken katsu curry

This dish is certainly an all-time favourite both in Japan and abroad. I remember hearing that it's one of the most popular Japanese dishes served in Japanese restaurants outside Japan. Here's my foolproof recipe so you can try it at home.

To make the curry sauce (takes about 15 minutes, not including time to make the roux on page 89):

1   If you are using ready-made curry roux, follow the pack instructions to make up.

2   For my home-made curry roux, place the roux and cold water in a saucepan and mix well with a whisk or fork before turning the heat to medium and cooking for about 10 minutes or until the sauce thickens to your liking (continue to stir while cooking).

To make the chicken katsu (breaded chicken breast) (takes about 15 minutes):

1   Cut the chicken breasts into a butterfly cut (this will allow the chicken to cook through faster in the oil).

2   Prepare the flour, beaten egg and panko on three separate plates. Then coat the chicken breasts in flour, dip in the beaten egg and cover in panko.

3   Heat enough oil for deep-frying in a heavy-based saucepan to 170°C. To check if the oil is hot enough, place a bit of panko into the oil. If it's the right temperature the panko will rise to the top of the oil, sizzle and fry but not brown immediately.

4   Gently place the breaded chicken breasts into the oil. Fry for a few minutes until the panko turns a nice golden brown colour and then turn over and fry for another few minutes.

5   Remove from the oil and place on kitchen paper.

6   Cut into thick slices while still hot.

7   Serve on a plate with the boiled rice, curry sauce and beni shoga.

Serves 2

For the chicken katsu (breaded chicken breast)

2 chicken breasts

flour for coating

1 egg, beaten

panko for coating

vegetable oil for frying

For the curry sauce

ready-made curry roux *or* Fiona's home-made Japanese curry roux (see page 89)

300ml cold water

To serve

boiled rice

beni shoga (red pickled ginger)

teriyaki chicken wings

This is a great recipe if you're entertaining at home, as you can marinate the chicken wings in advance and then just put them in the oven or on the barbeque. This recipe is loved by both adults and kids and there are never any leftovers!

Serves 6

1kg chicken wings

For the marinade

4 tablespoons soy sauce

4 tablespoons maple syrup

1 teaspoon sesame oil

1 teaspoon shichimi togarashi

1   In a large bowl mix together all the ingredients for the marinade until the maple syrup has dissolved.

2   Add the chicken wings and evenly coat in the marinade. Put in a sealed bag or container and store in the fridge for a few hours or overnight.

3   Cook in a fan oven for about 25 minutes at 180°C or until the chicken is cooked. (To check if the chicken is cooked cut one wing open and if the meat is white then it is ready.) Turn the chicken wings a few times during cooking.

✳   Tip

Add more shichimi togarashi if you like your chicken wings more spicy.

BEEF, PORK & LAMB

Historically in Japan there was a social taboo about eating meat due to the Buddhist belief of reincarnation. However, this doesn't exist in modern Japan and most people enjoy eating meat. Japan has become well known across the world for its Wagyu beef (also called Kobe beef). Wagyu is a Japanese breed of beef famous for its intense marbling, great taste and higher price tag. Recent studies have proved that the monounsaturated fats in Wagyu beef can actually help to lower cholesterol, which makes Wagyu far healthier than any other beef product. Thanks to Pat Whelan, a well-known Irish butcher, we can enjoy a type of Wagyu beef here in Ireland called 'Whelan Wagyu', which is a cross-breed of Japanese Wagyu and Pat's own Aberdeen Angus.

Across Japan you can find an interesting array of restaurants each specialising in one type of food. When my husband and I lived in Japan we loved eating out with friends at Japanese barbeque restaurants called 'Yakiniku-ya'. These restaurants can be found all over Japan and offer 'all you can eat and/or drink' for a set price, so needless to say we always arrived very hungry! My favourite thing about yakiniku restaurants is that you can order a selection of thinly cut raw meats from the menu along with vegetables and then cook these for yourself at your table on a built-in grill. The dipping sauces that they serve with the meat are called 'tare' and are so tasty. All the meat is bite-sized, so it's easy to eat with chopsticks.

In this chapter I share my family's favourite meat recipes, from my husband's Japanese-style burger to my freezer-friendly one-pot dishes and Japanese stews to get you through the autumn and winter months.

gilmar's japanese-style burger

This is my husband Gilmar's recipe. The sweet Japanese sauce mixed with the beef mince makes this burger really moist and tasty. You can enjoy it with a breaded bun, although traditionally burgers in Japan are served with plain white rice and steamed vegetables. If you want to serve cheese with this burger use a light-flavoured cheese such as edam (avoid cheddar).

Makes 4–5 burgers

4 tablespoons ketchup

1 tablespoon sake

1 tablespoon soy sauce

2 tablespoons Worcestershire sauce

1 egg, beaten

300g good quality beef mince

1 small red chilli, seeds removed and finely diced

40g panko

vegetable oil

To serve

buns

tomato

mixed leaves

edam cheese, sliced (optional)

mayonnaise

1   Preheat a fan oven to 180°C.

2   Mix the ketchup, sake, soy sauce and Worcestershire sauce in a bowl. Transfer half of the sauce to another bowl and set aside.

3   Add the beaten egg to the remaining half of the sauce in the bowl and mix well.

4   Toss in the beef mince, chilli and panko and mix well.

5   Using your hands, shape the meat mix into burger patties. This should make four or five depending on the size.

6   Brush the baking tray and the burgers with vegetable oil. Put the burgers on the baking tray and place in the preheated oven.

7   Cook for about 25 minutes, turning only once during this time and pouring the remaining half of the sauce over the top of the burgers in the last 5 minutes of cooking.

8   Serve in a bun with tomato, lettuce and mayonnaise.

✷ Tip

Put the burgers in the fridge for 30 minutes before cooking to help make the patties firm.

teriyaki steak with lotus-root chips

I've added a Japanese twist to a regular pan-fried steak by adding one of my favourite Japanese sauces, teriyaki. This is a really quick recipe to cook at home in the evening after work. When you're finished cooking the steak you can continue to cook the remaining sauce on the pan until its consistency resembles that of syrup and then pour this over the steak when serving.

1   Prepare the lotus-root chips (see page 100).

2   Take the steaks out of the fridge and leave to rest for about 10 minutes.

3   Mix all the ingredients for the teriyaki sauce in a bowl and set aside.

4   Using your hands, rub a little vegetable oil all over the steaks.

5   Heat a large, heavy-based frying pan over a high heat and place the steaks on the pan, searing both sides.

6   Pour the teriyaki sauce over the steaks and continue to fry for a few minutes on each side or until the steak is cooked to your liking. (While cooking the steaks use a spoon to continuously cover them with the teriyaki sauce sitting in the pan.)

7   Serve on a plate and drizzle the remaining teriyaki sauce in the frying pan over the steaks.

8   Garnish with finely sliced spring onion and sesame seeds.

Serves 2

2 steaks, ribeye or striploin

vegetable oil

spring onion to garnish

sesame seeds to garnish

Teriyaki sauce

4 tablespoons soy sauce

2 tablespoons sake

2 tablespoons mirin

1 teaspoon honey/sugar

lotus-root chips

Lotus root is a popular Asian vegetable which is renowned for its beauty and health benefits, including aiding digestion, increasing energy levels, improving the immune function, regulating blood pressure and treating lung-related illnesses. It's widely used in cooking across Asia, but outside Japan you may have to go to Asian speciality stores to find it. In the West it's often served as a garnish or on the side due to the beautiful appearance of the lotus root once it's cut. These chips work well as a snack/finger food, or as an accompaniment to a main meal.

Serves 2

1 large fresh lotus root

1 teaspoon rice vinegar

bowl of water for soaking

a mix of vegetable oil and sesame oil at a ratio of 3:1 for deep-frying

salt and pepper to season

1   Peel the lotus root and finely slice using a sharp knife or mandolin.

2   Add the vinegar/lemon juice to a bowl of water.

3   Place the sliced lotus root in the bowl of water for about 5 minutes. This will stop the lotus root from browning.

4   Pat the lotus root dry with kitchen paper.

5   Heat the oils to 170°C in a saucepan. To check if the oil is at the right temperature just place one of the lotus-root slices in it. If it pops to the top of the oil and starts sizzling then the oil is at the right temperature.

6   Fry the lotus-root slices in the oil until they turn a nice golden-brown colour.

7   Place on kitchen paper to absorb any excess oil, then season with salt and pepper and serve.

✳ Tip

You can use white-wine vinegar or lemon juice instead of the rice vinegar.

tonjiru
miso stew with pork & local vegetables

This is a hearty dish that uses local root vegetables along with pork and miso paste. It's perfect for a cold autumn or winter's day.

1   Heat the vegetable oil in a large, heavy-based saucepan and fry the pork slices until browned on both sides.

2   Pour the sake over the meat and then add the turnip, carrot and potato to the pan. Stir and continue to fry for a few minutes.

3   Pour the dashi into the saucepan with the meat and vegetables, and bring to the boil.

4   Reduce to a simmer and, using a ladle, skim the surface of the water, removing any foam that floats to the top.

5   Cover with a lid and cook on a low heat for about 30 minutes or until the vegetables are cooked through.

6   Dilute the miso paste in a small cup of dashi taken from the saucepan, then add to the saucepan and gently stir until mixed through. Do not allow to boil once the miso is added.

7   Serve in a bowl and garnish with sliced spring onion and shichimi togarashi if you'd like to add a little spice.

Serves 4

vegetable oil

200g pork steak, thinly sliced

1 tablespoon sake

1 small turnip (200g), peeled and roughly chopped

1 medium carrot (100g), peeled and roughly chopped

1 medium potato (150g), peeled and roughly chopped

1 litre dashi (see pages 52–54 for home-made dashi or for instant dashi use 1 litre of water and 1 teaspoon of dashi granules)

2–3 tablespoons miso paste, depending on taste

spring onion to garnish

shichimi togarashi to garnish

nikujaga
beef & potato stew

Thinly sliced beef is traditionally used for this recipe, but I'm using beef mince as I love the way it absorbs the sweet and savoury flavours of the sauce. I loved cooking this recipe when I lived in Japan as it reminded me a little of an Irish stew.

Serves 3–4

vegetable oil

1 large onion (150g), peeled and roughly chopped

250g good quality beef mince

1 tablespoon freshly grated ginger

1 large carrot (150g), peeled and roughly chopped

2 large potatoes (400g), peeled and roughly chopped

blanched green beans to serve

bowls of boiled rice with peas to serve

For the broth

500ml dashi (see pages 52–54)

80ml soy sauce

2 tablespoons sake

1 tablespoon mirin

1 tablespoon sugar

1 Heat the oil in a large, heavy-based saucepan on a medium to high heat.

2 Add the onion and fry for a minute or so. Then add the beef mince and ginger and continue to fry for a few more minutes.

3 Toss in the carrot and potatoes.

4 Mix all the ingredients for the broth together in a large bowl and then add to the saucepan.

5 Bring to the boil and then reduce to a simmer.

6 Using a ladle remove any foam that floats to the top of the water.

7 Cover with a lid and cook on a low heat for about 30 minutes or until the vegetables are cooked through.

8 Serve in a bowl and top with thinly sliced blanched green beans, accompanied by bowls of boiled rice with peas.

✳ Tip

If you want to freeze this dish you should remove the cooked potatoes first as they don't freeze well.

tonkatsu
fried panko pork

This recipe is similar to chicken katsu (see page 91) except that pork is used instead. Tonkatsu is usually served with tonkatsu sauce drizzled over it and a shredded-cabbage and tomato side salad.

Serves 2

2 pork chops/cutlets

salt and pepper to season

plain flour for coating

1 egg, beaten

panko for coating

vegetable oil for deep-frying

white cabbage to serve

tomato wedges to serve

Home-made tonkatsu sauce

3 tablespoons tomato ketchup

4 tablespoons water

3 tablespoons Worcestershire sauce

1 tablespoon sake or red wine

1 tablespoon soy sauce

1 teaspoon sugar

1   To make the home-made tonkatsu sauce, put all the ingredients in a saucepan and simmer for about 10 minutes until the sauce thickens to the same consistency as tomato ketchup, then set aside.

2   Using a sharp knife make small cuts about one inch apart all around the fatty edge of the pork chops to keep the chop flat when deep-frying (cut the fat off the pork chops if you prefer).

3   Season the pork chops with salt and pepper and coat in flour, shaking off any excess.

4   Dip in the beaten egg and finally coat in panko, using your hands to lightly press the panko onto the pork chops.

5   Heat the oil in a heavy-based saucepan to 170°C. Place a bit of panko into the oil to check if it is hot enough. If the panko rises to the top and starts to sizzle, then the oil is at the right temperature.

6   Gently place the breaded pork chop into the oil. Fry for a few minutes until the panko turns a nice golden-brown colour, then turn and fry for a few more minutes.

7   Remove the pork chop from the oil and place on kitchen paper.

8   Cut into thick slices while still hot.

9   Serve on a bed of finely cut white cabbage and tomato wedges. Drizzle the tonkatsu sauce over the breaded pork chops.

beef mince &
aubergine teriyaki

This is a really quick one-pot dish which you can leave simmering while you work away on something else or just relax! The beef mince and aubergine are really tender and sweet after being simmered in the teriyaki sauce.

1   Mix the ingredients for the teriyaki sauce together in a small bowl until the sugar is dissolved, then set aside.

2   Heat the vegetable oil in a medium-sized saucepan over a medium heat.

3   Add the ginger and garlic and fry for a minute or so (do not brown the garlic or ginger).

4   Add the mince and stir using a wooden spoon to help break up the mince. Continue to fry until the meat is nearly cooked (do not cook the meat fully or it may become dry).

5   Add the aubergine pieces and stir into the mince using the wooden spoon.

6   Pour the teriyaki sauce over the mince and aubergine and mix well together. Cook on a high heat for a few minutes, then let it simmer until the aubergine is tender and most of the liquid has been absorbed.

7   Serve with boiled rice and cooked garden peas.

Serves 4

1 tablespoon vegetable oil

2 inches ginger root, peeled and finely chopped

2 large cloves of garlic, peeled and finely chopped

450g good quality beef mince

2 large aubergines (cut into large, square pieces)

4 portions of boiled rice to serve

A few handfuls of cooked garden peas to serve

Teriyaki sauce

8 tablespoons soy sauce

4 tablespoons mirin

4 tablespoons sake

2 teaspoons sugar

✳   Tip

This dish can be kept in the fridge for a few days and freezes really well.

okonomiyaki
japanese-style pancake

Okonomiyaki is a popular street food in Japan. This recipe brings me back to one of my first dates with my husband Gilmar. We went to a Japanese food festival (matsuri) and ordered it. I remember thinking that it tasted so good it would be impossible to try to make it at home. But after many trials in my kitchen I've created a recipe that's so easy to make anybody could do it. When we eat this at home together I always fondly remember our time in Japan.

1   Put all the ingredients for the okonomiyaki sauce in a saucepan and leave to simmer for about 10 minutes until it thickens to the same consistency as tomato ketchup, then set aside and allow to cool.

2   Place the shredded cabbage and spring onions in a large bowl and completely coat in flour.

3   Whisk the eggs and dashi together in a jug. Pour over the cabbage and mix well together.

4   Heat some oil in a large, non-stick frying pan on a medium to high heat.

5   For one pancake, completely cover the base of the frying pan with half the bacon slices in a single layer, and fry for a few minutes.

6   Carefully place half of the cabbage mix on top of the layer of bacon.

7   Fry for a few more minutes, then, if you are not confident enough to flip the pancake, do the following: place a large plate over the frying pan and turn the pancake onto the plate. Add more oil to the frying pan. Carefully slide the pancake off the plate and onto the frying pan with the uncooked part facing down.

8   Continue to fry for less than 5 minutes on a medium to low heat. When ready, place on a serving plate with the bacon side of the pancake facing up.

9   Using the back of a spoon or a small brush, cover the top of the pancake with the okonomiyaki sauce. Decorate with lines of mayonnaise in a criss-cross design and then sprinkle milled seaweed, beni shoga and katsuobushi on top as shown in the picture.

Serves 4 (makes 2 pancakes)

250g savoy cabbage, finely shredded

2 spring onions, finely cut diagonally

100g plain flour

4 eggs

200ml dashi (instant p. 50 or home-made p. 54)

vegetable oil

6–8 slices of bacon/rashers, depending on the size of the frying pan

For the okonomiyaki sauce

3 tablespoons tomato ketchup

4 tablespoons water

3 tablespoons Worcestershire sauce

1 tablespoon sake or red wine

1 tablespoon soy sauce

1 teaspoon sugar

To serve

mayonnaise (preferably in a tube so you can decorate the top with lines)

milled nori or dillisk seaweed

beni shoga (pickled red ginger) (optional)

katsuobushi (dried fish flakes) (optional)

shichimi lamb kofta kebabs

Sheep are a big part of Irish culture and heritage. As a nation, we're very proud of our lamb meat and it's exported all over the world. I was brought up on a sheep farm, so needless to say I ate a lot of lamb during my childhood. So for these reasons I had to dedicate at least one recipe to lamb. I season the lamb meat with shichimi togarashi (Japanese seven spice) and serve it with a natural yoghurt dip, as we have fantastic yoghurt producers in Ireland who make excellent quality yoghurt.

Makes 8 skewers

vegetable oil

1 medium onion, peeled and finely diced

500g good quality lamb, minced

bunch of fresh parsley, finely chopped

1 tablespoon shichimi togarashi

salt and pepper to season

8 skewers, soaked in water for 20 minutes

Yoghurt and mint dip

5 tablespoons natural yoghurt

large bunch of mint leaves, finely chopped

2 teaspoons lime juice

zest of ½ a lime

1 teaspoon olive oil

salt and pepper to season

1   Heat the oil in a frying pan on a medium heat and add the diced onion. Slowly cook the onion, allowing it to sweat, and then fry until translucent (do not brown). Remove from the heat and let it cool.

2   In a large bowl mix together the minced lamb, parsley, shichimi togarashi and onion. Season with salt and pepper.

3   With dampened hands take a handful of meat and using a firm hand form a rectangular shape. Push a skewer through the meat.

4   Place under a grill on a high heat for 10 to 20 minutes (or until cooked to your liking). Place a cup of water on the base of the grill to stop the meat drying out.

5   Mix all the ingredients for the dip together in a bowl and serve on the side.

FISH & SEAFOOD

The Japanese diet is rich in fish and seafood. Slices of raw fish
called 'sashimi' are eaten as part of the Japanese diet. Fish is also
cooked in various ways when served with a main meal, such as
grilling, poaching and steaming. Most Japanese homes don't have
Western-style ovens; instead they have small electric grills, so
they tend to grill fish at home.

    Although both Japan and Ireland are island nations, the
Japanese are much more adventurous when it comes to eating
fish and seafood. My Japanese friends were surprised to hear that
Irish people eat more meat than fish. However, Ireland is changing
and people are starting to eat more types of fish.

    When my sister came to visit me in Japan, my boss wanted
to welcome her to our local village by bringing us to a traditional
Japanese restaurant. My sister was not prepared for the menu of
fish and seafood, most of which were unfamiliar to her, such as
squid, octopus, shellfish, eel and sea urchin! She attempted to eat
some of the dishes to be polite, but she's never forgiven me for
this!

    The recipes in this chapter include a mix of traditional Japanese
recipes, such as saba shioyaki (grilled mackerel) and salmon
teriyaki, and then fusion recipes that I have created, such as
Uyema's spicy crab and rice cakes.

salmon teriyaki

Without exception, everyone loves this recipe – it's one of the most talked about recipes at my cooking classes. The perfect combination of flavours in the salmon and the sweet teriyaki sauce make this an all-time favourite in households across the world and on menus in both Asian and non-Asian restaurants.

Serves 2

vegetable oil

2 fillets salmon

handful of sesame seeds to garnish

Teriyaki sauce

4 tablespoons soy sauce

2 tablespoons sake

2 tablespoons mirin

1 teaspoon sugar/honey

1   Combine all the ingredients for the teriyaki sauce, mix well and set aside.

2   Pour a little vegetable oil into a non-stick frying pan on a medium to high heat.

3   Place the salmon fillets (skin-side down) on the frying pan and sear both sides of the fish.

4   When the fish is nearly cooked (place the salmon fillets skin-side down at this point) pour the teriyaki sauce over it.

5   Use a large spoon to continually pour the sauce over the fish fillets while continuing to fry.

6   Fry until the teriyaki sauce is reduced to the consistency of a syrup.

7   Garnish with sesame seeds.

✳   Tip

Keep a close eye on the teriyaki sauce as it can quickly reduce on a high heat and start to burn.

seabass tempura goujons

Tempura batter is light and crispy compared to the Western-style batter with which we are familiar and which can be heavy and doughy. You can use any type of white fish for this recipe. Make sure to remove all bones from the fish fillet before making the goujons.

1 Coat the seabass pieces in cornflour seasoned with salt and pepper and shake off any excess. Set aside.

2 Before you start to make the tempura batter have everything ready to go (i.e. oil in the saucepan, plate lined with kitchen paper, tongs to take the fish out of the oil). It's important to use the batter mix as soon as it's made so you get a light and crispy batter.

3 Beat the egg yolk and ice-cold water in a large bowl. Toss in a few ice cubes to keep the water cold.

4 Mix the flour and cornflour together in a separate bowl, then add to the water/egg mixture. Using your hand, lightly mix. It's OK to leave lumps in the batter (do not overmix as this will make the batter heavy and doughy).

5 Heat the oil in a large, heavy-based saucepan to 170°C. Drop a bit of batter into the oil to check the temperature. If the batter rises slowly to the top of the oil, starts to sizzle and slowly turns a golden-brown colour, then the temperature is right.

6 Dip one of the seabass pieces in the batter mix.

7 Carefully place in the oil and fry until golden-brown, turning a few times. Continue to do this until all the pieces are deep-fried (do not overcrowd the pan as the oil temperature will drop).

8 Drain on kitchen paper to absorb any excess oil.

9 Mix the mayonnaise and wasabi in a small serving bowl and serve along with the goujons. Garnish with lemon wedges and freshly ground sea salt.

Serves 2

2 seabass fillets, cut into thick strips
cornflour to coat

For the batter

1 egg yolk

100ml ice-cold water

a few ice cubes

75g flour, sieved

25g cornflour, sieved

salt and pepper to season

vegetable oil for deep-frying

lemon wedges and freshly ground sea salt to garnish

Dip

4 tablespoons mayonnaise

1 teaspoon wasabi

ebi furai
fried panko prawns

This recipe can be served as a main meal alongside a side salad of shredded cabbage with tomato and boiled rice. Alternatively, it can be served as a finger food when entertaining at home. The prawns can be prepared in advance and stored in the fridge, then deep-fried when everyone is ready to eat!

Serves 2–4 (makes 12 panko prawns)

12 large uncooked prawns

plain flour to coat

1–2 eggs (depending on prawn size), beaten and seasoned with salt and pepper

panko to coat

vegetable oil for deep-frying

To serve

shredded cabbage

tomato wedges

lemon wedges

1 To de-shell the prawns, pull off the head and legs with your fingers, and peel away the shell. Do not remove the tails as they look nicer with the tails attached.

2 To de-vein the prawns, check to see if there's a black line running down the back of the prawn. If so, remove using a toothpick. This can be eaten, but the prawn tastes and looks better without it.

3 Wash the prawns under a cold running tap and pat dry with kitchen paper.

4 To straighten the prawns (and to avoid them curling when frying) make a few incisions in the belly starting in the middle and working towards the tail.

5 Place the flour, beaten egg and panko on three separate plates.

6 Coat the prawns in flour, then egg and finally in panko. Use your hands to lightly press the panko onto the prawns.

7 In a large, heavy-based saucepan, heat the oil to 170°C. Check the oil temperature by placing some panko in the oil. If the panko floats to the top of the oil and sizzles, turning a golden brown colour slowly, then it's at the right temperature. If the panko turns a golden brown colour immediately, the oil is too hot.

8 Gently place the panko-coated prawns in the oil and deep-fry for a few minutes or until golden brown. To avoid the oil temperature dropping don't overcrowd the pan.

9 Arrange the cooked prawns on kitchen paper to absorb any excess oil.

10 Serve the panko prawns with shredded cabbage, tomato and lemon wedges.

uyema's spicy crab & rice cakes

For this recipe I mix the crab meat with Japanese rice, the sticky texture of which helps to hold the cake together. If you're making these for kids you can make the patties smaller and either reduce or leave out the chilli.

1   Add the cooked rice, crab meat, ginger, chilli and parsley to a large bowl. Season with salt and pepper. Using your hands mix all the ingredients together well.

2   Using dampened hands take one-quarter of the rice and crab mix and roll it in the shape of a ball. Then, using your hands, flatten the ball and press firmly to make the shape of a patty.

3   Lightly dust the patties in flour, shaking off any excess.

4   Heat some vegetable oil in a non-stick frying pan over a medium heat and fry the patties for about 5 minutes on each side until golden brown.

5   Mix the sour cream, lemon juice, salt and pepper together in a small bowl.

6   Serve the crab cakes with the dip and lemon wedges.

✳ Tip

Put the crab cakes in the fridge for 30 minutes before frying to help firm them up.

Makes 4 crab cakes

140g cooked Japanese rice (80g uncooked rice), cold or hot

140g good quality cooked crab meat

1 tablespoon freshly grated ginger

1 medium fresh red chilli (seeds removed), finely chopped

1 tablespoon flat-leaf parsley, finely chopped

salt and pepper to season

bowl of water to dampen your hands

flour for dusting

vegetable oil

a few lemon wedges to serve

Dip

100ml sour cream

juice of ½ a lemon

salt and pepper to season

saba shioyaki
grilled salted mackerel

This dish reminds me a little of Portuguese salted sardines. Traditionally, saba shioyaki is grilled, but I prefer to pan-fry it. The mackerel is so full of flavour that it can be eaten with just plain rice or it can be served with soy sauce drizzled over grated daikon (mooli). Daikon is a radish that resembles a large white carrot. If you can't find daikon for this recipe you can use ginger instead.

Serves 2

2 fresh mackerel fillets

sea salt, freshly ground

vegetable oil

To serve

soy sauce

freshly grated ginger or daikon (mooli)

1   Generously season the mackerel fillets with sea salt on both sides and set aside.

2   Pour some vegetable oil into a non-stick frying pan and set the heat at medium to high.

3   Once the pan is hot, place the mackerel fillets into it skin-side down and fry for a few minutes depending on the size. Then turn over and cook the other side for another few minutes until cooked through. The skin should be nice and crispy.

4   Serve with soy sauce drizzled over either freshly grated ginger or daikon.

✳   Tip

If you have time, leave the salt on the fish for 10–20 minutes. Pat dry with kitchen paper before frying.

japanese-style oysters

In Ireland we are blessed with an abundance of oysters, which have become closely associated with Irish heritage. So much so that one of Ireland's largest festivals is dedicated to this delicacy – the 'Galway International Oyster and Seafood Festival'. Every year people travel from all over the world to attend this amazing festival, where they can enjoy Irish music and dance, along with fresh Irish oysters, and witness the world's oyster opening championship.

You don't need to do much with oysters, just add a little gentle seasoning.

1   Using a tea towel and a small sharp knife, open the oysters.

2   Pour some freshly squeezed lemon juice over the oysters and serve with beni shoga, shichimi togarashi and soy sauce.

3   Place them on a large serving dish with crushed ice.

Serves 2

12 fresh oysters

freshly squeezed lemon juice

beni shoga (pickled red ginger), finely chopped

shichimi togarashi (Japanese seven spice)

soy sauce

crushed ice to serve

✳ Tip

Make sure to source really fresh oysters from a reliable fishmonger.

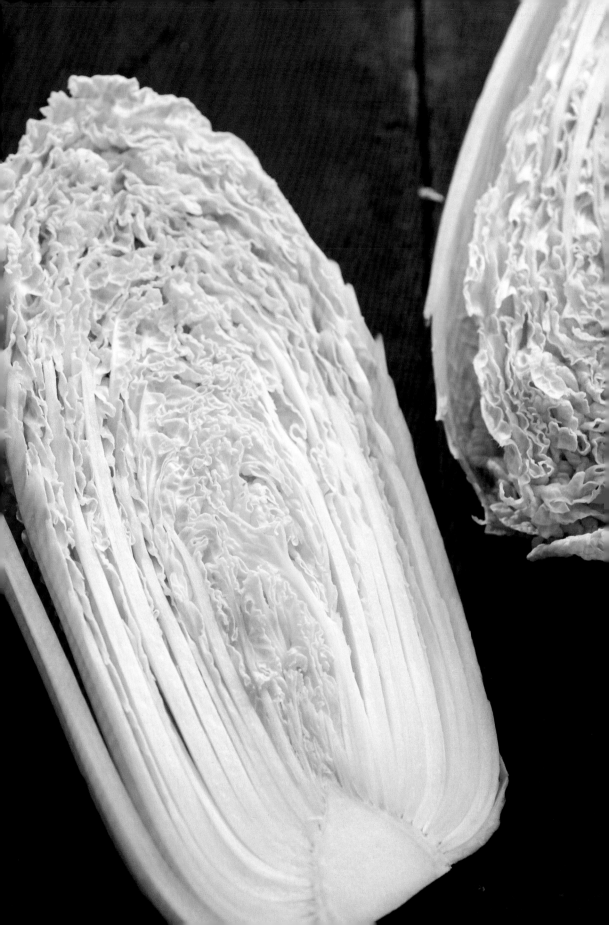

VEGETARIAN

In this chapter I focus on some of my favourite Japanese vegetarian foods, including edamame (soybeans in a pod) and tofu. There's also a selection of vegetarian side dishes that can be served with a bowl of rice and miso soup. My favourite treat in this chapter is the kakiage (mixed vegetable tempura). You have to try this!

A vegetarian option is generally included as part of a Japanese meal to maintain the balance. If you are a vegetarian eating in Japan or in a Japanese restaurant, don't assume that a vegetarian dish has no meat or fish, as the stock used to flavour the dish may contain either.

While this chapter is dedicated to vegetarian dishes, you can find more vegetarian recipes throughout the book. In the chapter on rice there are vegetarian recipes, including seasoned boiled rice, fried rice and rice balls. In the soups and salad chapter there are recipes for Japanese cooking stock and miso soup filled with the vitamins and minerals from seaweed needed for a vegetarian diet. There are also a few salad recipes which can be eaten as a main course or a starter. The chicken gyoza recipe works really well with vegetables only and some of my stew recipes can be adapted for vegetarians by replacing the meat with beans. Finally, any of the sushi included in this book can be easily adapted to include a selection of vegetarian ingredients including avocado, mango, cucumber and peppers.

edamame

Edamame are young soybeans in a pod. I loved this popular snack when I first moved to Japan as a student, as they are really cheap to buy and tasty, and go surprisingly well with beer. Generally, edamame can be found in the frozen section of Asian speciality stores or larger supermarkets. They are sold in the pod and also out of the pod. I prefer using edamame in the pod when serving as a simple snack or finger food and then using edamame out of the pod for when I'm making a dish with them.

To cook frozen pre-cooked edamame, place them in a large bowl and completely cover with boiling water. Leave for a few minutes, then drain. Fresh raw edamame should be cooked in a saucepan of boiling water for about 5 minutes and then drained.

Serve edamame with an empty bowl to dispose of the pods. Remember you can't eat the pods! Check to see if the edamame have been pre-salted or not and then season to your liking with freshly ground sea salt. To eat edamame simply pop the beans out of the pod using either your hands or your mouth. To add a nice kick to your cooked edamame sprinkle with shichimi togarashi (Japanese seven spice) or just cayenne pepper.

edamame hummus

Apart from eating them directly from the pods, there are lots of other different ways that you can use edamame, such as tossing the beans into salads and stir-fries. This recipe is one of my favourite ways to use edamame.

Serves 2–3

1 tablespoon sesame seeds

200g edamame (out of the pod)

2 tablespoons olive oil

½ teaspoon sesame oil

½ clove of garlic, crushed

juice of 1 lemon

2 tablespoons water

freshly ground salt and pepper to season

You'll need

pestle and mortar

blender

1   Toss the sesame seeds into a roasting tray and place in a fan oven preheated to 150°C for about 5 minutes.

2   Using a pestle and mortar, grind the hot sesame seeds until most of them are cracked and ground.

3   Cook the edamame, then drain. If still in the pods, remove by using your fingers to gently squeeze the beans out.

4   Place the cooked edamame beans, ground sesame seeds and the remaining ingredients in a blender and blitz until the texture is nice and creamy.

5   If you think the mixture is too dry, then add a little more olive oil or water.

✷   Tip

Serve with pitta bread or raw vegetable sticks.

tofu

Tofu is a soybean product which is low in calories yet high in protein and calcium. The quality and taste of some of the packed tofu available in the West are poor and some tofu products are made from genetically modified soybeans, so make sure to buy good quality GM-free/organic tofu to get a real sense of how great it can taste. I tend to buy tofu products with a short best before date, usually one or two weeks.

The two main types of tofu are silken and firm. Silken tofu is very soft and delicate, and firm tofu, as the name suggests, is a little firmer in texture. Both can be used in different types of cooking depending on which you prefer, but silken tends to go best in soups and salads and firm tofu works better in stir-fries.

hiyayakko
cold tofu salad

Fresh tofu can be eaten cold straight from the fridge and it was one of the first Japanese dishes I prepared at home. I couldn't believe how well the plain tofu absorbed the intense flavours of the freshly grated ginger, spring onion and soy sauce. This is great served as a side dish or starter. For non-vegetarians this dish is also very nice with a handful of katsuobushi/ bonito fish flakes added with the ginger and spring onion.

Serves 2

1 pack of cold silken tofu
(preferably GM free)

1 thumb-size piece of freshly
grated ginger

handful of spring onion, finely
chopped

3 teaspoons soy sauce

1   Gently drain the water from the block of tofu, using kitchen paper to absorb the excess, and place on a serving plate.

2   Place the grated ginger and spring onion on top of the tofu.

3   Drizzle soy sauce over the tofu and toppings just before serving.

✳ Tip

You can serve this dish Japanese style as one block of tofu and let everyone help themselves, or you can cut the tofu into smaller blocks and put a little topping on each small block, then serve on individual plates.

tofu & mixed vegetable stir-fry

I love stir-fries because they are something you can throw together after a busy day at work with leftover vegetables from the fridge. All you need for this recipe is a block of tofu! I've listed recommended vegetables, but feel free to add whatever is in the fridge.

1   Heat equal amounts of the vegetable oil and sesame oil in a large frying pan/wok on a high heat.

2   Toss in the ginger and fry for less than a minute (do not brown). Then add the carrots and mushrooms, followed by the remaining vegetables and mix well together for a few minutes.

3   Cut the tofu into cubes and add to the pan, followed by the sake and soy sauce.

4   Continue to fry and mix together for another minute, then take off the heat and serve.

5   Garnish with sesame seeds.

✳ Tip

   Be gentle when mixing the stir-fry, as the tofu can break apart easily.

Serves 2

vegetable oil

sesame oil

thumb-size piece of ginger (20g), peeled and finely chopped

100g carrots, peeled and cut julienne style

100g mushrooms, roughly chopped

75g mangetout peas

100g beansprouts

100g baby corn

100g tofu (preferably GM free)

2 tablespoons sake

1 tablespoon soy sauce

Garnish

mixed sesame seeds

tofu nuggets

This is a nice recipe for party finger food, for a tasty snack to enjoy at home or for a packed lunch.

1   To remove the excess water from the block of tofu, wrap it in kitchen paper and set aside for 10 minutes. You can place a weight (such as a book) on top of the block of tofu to help the water drain faster.

2   Mix the panko and the dillisk together and transfer to a flat plate.

3   Place the beaten egg on a flat plate.

4   Remove the kitchen paper from the tofu and, using a sharp knife, cut it into small bite-size cubes.

5   Coat all the tofu cubes in egg, then in the panko mix and arrange on a large plate.

6   Add some vegetable oil to a large non-stick frying pan and set the heat to medium.

7   Carefully place all the tofu nuggets on the pan and fry until each side is slightly browned and crispy (add more oil to the pan as you turn the tofu nuggets if necessary).

8   To make the dip simply mix the wasabi and mayonnaise in a small bowl and serve.

Serves 4

300g tofu

50g panko

1 teaspoon milled dillisk (optional)

1 egg, beaten

vegetable oil

Dip

1 tablespoon wasabi paste

4 tablespoons mayonnaise

kakiage

mixed vegetable tempura

I was lucky to learn the secret to a light and crispy tempura batter while living in Japan and it's simple – don't overmix the batter and use ice-cold water. Overmixing the batter will activate the gluten, leaving the batter heavy and doughy, so lumps are OK.

Serves 4

vegetable oil for deep-frying

lemon wedges to serve

freshly ground sea salt to serve (optional)

For the vegetable mix

80g sweet potato, cut into matchsticks with the skin still on

80g carrots, peeled and cut into matchsticks

50g kale, stalk removed and roughly chopped

100g onion, peeled and cut into thin strips

2 tablespoons cornflour

For the batter

1 egg yolk

200ml ice-cold water

a few ice cubes

150g flour, sieved

50g cornflour, sieved

For the dipping sauce

100ml dashi stock (home-made dashi stock (pages 52–54) or 100ml water and a sprinkle of dashi instant granules)

20ml mirin

20ml soy sauce

grated ginger/daikon (optional)

1   Put all the ingredients for the dipping sauce into a saucepan and let them simmer for a few minutes, then set aside and let cool.

2   Mix all the vegetables in a large bowl and, using your hands, evenly coat them in cornflour, then set aside.

3   Beat the egg yolk and ice-cold water in a large bowl. Toss in a few ice cubes to keep the water cold.

4   Gradually add the flour and cornflour to the water/egg mix and then lightly mix. It's OK to leave lumps in the batter.

5   Toss all the vegetables into the batter mix and ensure they are all equally coated.

6   Heat the oil in a large, heavy-based saucepan to 170°C (medium/high heat). Drop a bit of batter in the oil to check the temperature. If the batter rises slowly to the top of the oil, starts to sizzle and slowly turns a golden-brown colour, then the temperature is right.

7   Put a large tablespoon of the tempura vegetable mix on a large wooden spoon and slowly place in the oil against the side of the saucepan. Use a large spoon or chopsticks to slide the tempura mix off the wooden spoon and into the oil. Remove the wooden spoon slowly once the tempura mix is secure and firmly bound together.

8   Deep-fry the tempura until it is golden brown, turning a few times.

9   Drain on kitchen paper to absorb any excess oil.

10 Serve with either the dipping sauce or lemon wedges and a sprinkle of freshly ground sea salt.

✳   Tips

For vegetarians use a vegetarian-based dashi stock using seaweed and/or shiitake mushrooms (see page 54).

Make sure none of the ice cubes are caught in the kakiage before you place it in the hot oil.

curried potato korroke (croquettes)

All types of korroke are popular in Japan and often found in shop-bought or home-made bentos. This is a great way to use leftover potatoes at home. Korroke are usually deep-fried, but I prefer to pan-fry them as it's healthier and they're just as tasty.

1   Heat some oil in a frying pan on a medium heat and add the onion. Slowly cook the onion, allowing it to sweat, then fry until translucent (do not brown).

2   In a large bowl mix the cooked onion, potato and curry powder.

3   Place the flour, beaten egg and panko on three separate plates.

4   Take a handful of potato mix and start to shape the potato into patty or oval shapes with your hands.

5   Coat each patty in the flour, egg and finally panko.

6   Pour a generous amount of oil into a frying pan on a medium heat.

7   Place the patties into the pan and fry on one side for about 5 minutes until golden brown. Then flip over and fry on the other side for a few more minutes until golden brown. Sit on kitchen paper to absorb any excess oil.

8   Serve with lime wedges.

Makes 6 patties

vegetable oil

1 small onion, peeled and finely diced

400g potatoes, boiled and mashed

1 tablespoon curry powder

flour for coating

1 egg, beaten

panko for coating

a few lime wedges to garnish

aubergine & ginger salad

The flavours in this salad are quite intense so it's best eaten on the side alongside other dishes, or with plain boiled rice. Although it can be eaten warm or cold, I prefer to eat it cold. It keeps well in the fridge for a few days as the flavours develop.

Serves 4

1 medium aubergine
(600/700g)

100ml water

Dressing

5ml sesame oil

50ml soy sauce

40ml vinegar

30g sugar

1 clove of garlic, peeled and finely chopped

1 tablespoon freshly grated ginger

1   In a large bowl, whisk all the ingredients for the dressing together until the sugar is dissolved, then set aside.

2   Cut the aubergine into thin slices. Heat the oil in a large frying pan on a medium to high heat and place the aubergine slices in a single layer, frying for about 2 minutes covered with a lid.

3   Add half of the water to the pan and cover with the lid again. Reduce the heat to medium. Fry until the water is fully absorbed.

4   If necessary put more oil in the frying pan when turning the aubergine slices and continue to fry for another 2 minutes with the lid on. Then add the remaining water to the pan and cover again, frying until the water is fully absorbed. If the aubergine is soft and cooked through at this stage, take off the heat. If the aubergine is not fully cooked (white in the middle), then continue to fry for a few more minutes.

5   Place the hot aubergine slices in the dressing and ensure that all the slices are well coated. Once cool place in a covered container in the fridge until serving.

hiroko's hakusai (asian cabbage) salad

My mother-in-law Hiroko is a fantastic cook and baker. She worked in her parents' bakery for many years. Although Hiroko was born in Brazil, both her parents came from Okinawa in Japan so her cooking is heavily influenced by the Japanese diet. Whenever my family and I travel to Brazil, we always look forward to her cooking. Due to the strong flavours in this dish Hiroko serves it on the side alongside other communal dishes, including rice, vegetables, fish or meat.

The salad can be eaten warm or cold, but I prefer to eat it straight from the fridge or at room temperature. It keeps well in the fridge for up to one week.

1   Wash each hakusai leaf carefully to remove any dirt.

2   Cut the leaves about 2 inches thick widthways.

3   Place the thicker leaf ends in boiling water for 2 minutes (these take a little longer to cook), then add the rest of the leaves for another minute. Drain the leaves in a colander and set aside to cool.

4   Put all the ingredients for the dressing in a small saucepan and bring to the boil, then immediately reduce to a very low heat. Stir to make sure the sugar is fully absorbed and continue to simmer on a very low heat.

5   In the meantime, carefully arrange the leaves so they are neatly aligned and upstanding in a dish with a flat base and sides. The leaves should fit tightly into the dish, as shown in the picture overleaf.

6   Pour the hot dressing evenly all over the leaves and scatter the chilli pieces on top. Garnish with the ginger slices.

7   Cover the dish with cling film and let it cool.

8   Put in the fridge for a few hours before serving.

Serves 4

250g hakusai (Asian cabbage)
a few thin slices of ginger to garnish

Dressing

dash of sesame oil

3 tablespoons sunflower oil

3 tablespoons sake

3 tablespoons soy sauce

25g sugar

25ml vinegar

pinch of salt

1 small chilli, roughly sliced with seeds removed

thumb-size piece of ginger, finely chopped

kale & garlic donburi

This recipe takes about 5 minutes to make (once the rice is cooked) and is packed with goodness. The flavour of the kale and garlic go really well with a bowl of plain boiled rice.

1   Cut the thick part of the stem from the kale leaves.

2   Roll the leaves into a bunch and cut into thin ribbons.

3   Pour the vegetable oil and olive oil into a non-stick frying pan.

4   Turn the heat to medium and toss the garlic in the pan, cooking until you start to get a nice aroma from the garlic (do not brown).

5   Season the garlic-infused oil with salt and pepper.

6   Add the chopped kale and reduce the heat to medium-low.

7   Pour the lemon juice over the kale.

8   Stir and fry until the kale is bright green all over.

9   At this point, take the kale off the hot pan as it will continue to cook.

10 Serve on top of a bowl of rice.

Serves 2

100g kale, washed

1 tablespoon vegetable oil

1 tablespoon olive oil

2 cloves of garlic, peeled and finely diced

salt and pepper to season

juice of ½ a lemon

2 portions of boiled rice to serve

cucumber & irish seaweed pickled salad

This is a refreshing side salad and is best served alongside other dishes.

Serves 6

handful of Irish seaweed

2 cucumbers

1 large carrot

For the dressing

100ml rice vinegar

3 teaspoons sugar

½ teaspoon salt

1   Put all the ingredients for the dressing in a clean empty jam jar or a small lunch box. Secure with a lid and shake the dressing a few times to allow the sugar to dissolve into the rice vinegar. Set aside.

2   Place the seaweed in water for 5–10 minutes to soften. Then use your hands to drain the excess water and pat dry with kitchen paper.

3   Cut the cucumbers in half. Use a tablespoon to take the seeds out of the middle (discard these), then thinly slice the cucumbers.

4   Use a peeler to make carrot ribbons.

5   Place all the ingredients in a large bowl.

6   Pour the dressing over the ingredients and mix well. Leave in the fridge for at least 20 minutes before serving. This can be stored in the fridge in an airtight container for one week.

NOODLES

Noodles were originally brought to Japan from China, but Japanese people loved them so much they integrated them into the Japanese diet, and noodle dishes such as ramen can now be called national dishes. The main types of noodles are ramen/egg, udon, somen and soba. Nowadays most of these can be found in large supermarkets, health stores and Asian speciality stores.

This chapter has a mix of dishes that can be thrown together quickly, such as the yakisoba with mixed vegetables, and dishes that require a little more time, such as ramen, which is going to be a real treat and definitely worth the effort. All of the recipes are very versatile and the ingredients can be easily replaced as long as the broth or sauce in the recipe is used.

home-made chicken stock

This recipe is similar to a standard chicken stock recipe but I've added a few ingredients to give a Japanese flavour and umami to the stock, including kombu (kelp) seaweed. After cooling the stock you can remove the thin layer of fat sitting on the surface of the liquid. Then it can be stored in the fridge for a few days or it can be frozen.

Makes 1 litre

1½ litres cold water

dried kombu (kelp), a postcard-sized piece

raw whole chicken carcass

1 large carrot, peeled and roughly chopped

1 leek, washed and roughly chopped

1 thumb-size piece of ginger, cut into slices

2 tablespoons sake (optional)

1   Place 1½ litres of cold water and dried kombu in a large saucepan. Set aside for at least 20 minutes to allow the water to absorb the umami from the seaweed.

2   Add the chicken carcass, carrot, leek, ginger and sake to the saucepan.

3   Bring to the boil and immediately reduce to a simmer.

4   Use a ladle to remove any foam from the top of the water and cover with a lid.

5   Continue to simmer for at least 1 hour and for up to 3 hours on a low–medium heat.

6   You should have a little over 1 litre of chicken stock left depending on how long it's been simmering.

7   Strain the stock through a sieve and allow to cool.

8   Store in the fridge for a few days or in the freezer for a few months.

chicken ramen

Ramen is one of the ultimate comfort foods. Although ramen is now part of the Japanese culture, it came originally from China. In Japan each ramen restaurant will have their own secret stock recipe and this is guarded from one generation to the next. You can find ramen stalls on street corners and these are popular places to visit on the way home after a night out.

1   To make the marinade for the chicken breast, in a small bowl mix together the sake, vegetable oil, salt and pepper.

2   Using your hands, completely cover the chicken in the marinade and leave to rest for 5 to 10 minutes.

3   Once the chicken is ready, heat a heavy-based pan on a medium to high heat and seal the chicken on both sides. Then reduce the heat and continue to fry until the chicken is cooked through, and set aside.

4   Bring the stock to the boil in a large saucepan and immediately reduce to a simmer.

5   Place the dried seaweed in a bowl of cold water for 5 minutes to soften. Then squeeze out any excess water and set aside.

6   Place the noodles in a bowl of boiling water and gently untangle using a fork or chopsticks. Drain in a colander and rinse under a running cold tap to remove any excess starch.

7   Toss the noodles into the stock. Bring the stock back to the boil, then immediately reduce to a simmer.

8   In a small bowl, mix the miso paste with a few tablespoons of hot stock from the saucepan, dissolving any lumps. Add the miso paste to the stock and mix well together.

9   Divide the noodles between two large serving bowls. Then divide the seaweed, beansprouts and pak choi evenly between the two bowls, arranging carefully. Slice the cooked chicken breast and place on top of the ingredients as shown in the picture.

10 Finally, fill the bowls about three-quarters full with the miso stock and garnish with spring onion and shichimi togarashi or chilli oil.

Serves 2

1 tablespoon sake

1 tablespoon vegetable oil

salt and pepper to season

1 chicken breast, butterfly cut

1 litre chicken stock (see recipe on page 154)

1 tablespoon dried seaweed

2 packs of egg or ramen noodles (about 400g)

3 tablespoons white miso paste

100g beansprouts, washed

handful of pak choi leaves, washed and roughly chopped

spring onion to garnish

shichimi togarashi and/or chilli oil to add a little spice

To serve ramen you'll need

2 large bowls

2 spoons

2 sets of chopsticks

yakisoba with mixed vegetables

For two years I lived in a beautiful rural village near the coast of Japan. Every summer the local community organised a trek, with a barbeque on the beach afterwards. I was surprised to see yakisoba being cooked on the barbeque, as usually you see it at street stalls during festivals. Of course you can also cook this dish at home too!

Serves 2

2 bundles or portions of egg or ramen noodles

vegetable oil

1 medium onion, peeled and finely sliced

2 cloves of garlic, peeled and finely diced

1 thumb-size piece of ginger, peeled and grated

large handful of savoy cabbage leaves, washed and finely chopped

2 medium carrots, peeled and cut julienne style

large handful of beansprouts, washed

For the sauce

3 tablespoons tomato ketchup

4 tablespoons water

3 tablespoons Worcestershire sauce

1 tablespoon sake or red wine

1 tablespoon soy sauce

1 teaspoon sugar

To garnish

milled dillisk or nori seaweed

beni shoga (red pickled ginger)

1 To make the home-made yakisoba sauce, put all the ingredients in a small saucepan and simmer for about 10 minutes on a medium heat until the sauce thickens to the same consistency as tomato ketchup and then set aside.

2 Cook the noodles according to the pack instructions, then set aside.

3 Heat some vegetable oil in a frying pan or wok and fry the onion for a minute. Then add the garlic and ginger along with the cabbage and fry for a minute or so before adding the carrots and beansprouts. Don't overcook the vegetables so they keep their crunchy texture.

4 Toss the noodles and sauce into the stir-fry and mix well, continuing to fry for a few minutes.

5 Serve on two plates and top with milled dillisk or nori seaweed and beni shoga.

✳ Tip

Remove the Worcestershire sauce to make this suitable for vegetarians.

curry udon noodles

This is a great recipe to use up leftover curry sauce. I often make this the day after making chicken katsu curry, as it means dinner just takes minutes to prepare with the leftover sauce! I'm adding mixed vegetables to this dish, but you can add just udon noodles or whatever you like. If you are making this recipe from scratch you can use either my home-made Japanese curry roux (on page 89) or a ready-made curry roux.

Serves 2

Fiona's home-made Japanese curry roux (see page 89)

500ml cold water

2 bundles or portions of udon noodles

a few handfuls of mushrooms, washed and roughly chopped

handful of baby sweetcorn, washed and roughly chopped

handful of mangetout, washed and roughly chopped

fresh ginger, finely chopped julienne style, to garnish

1 Place the curry roux and cold water in a saucepan on a medium heat and mix well with a whisk or fork. Bring to the boil and then reduce to a simmer for about 15 minutes or until it's thickened to your liking (stirring intermittently).

2 Cook the udon noodles according to the pack instructions. Then, along with the vegetables, add to the curry. Continue to simmer for a few more minutes.

3 Divide evenly between bowls, garnish and serve.

somen noodles &
prawn miso salad

This is a nice spring or summer salad recipe that can be thrown together in no time at all. The miso salad dressing for this recipe tastes best freshly made, so make it just before serving.

1   Put all the ingredients for the salad dressing in a bowl and mix well together using a whisk or fork. Then set aside.

2   Cook the noodles according to the pack instructions. Once cooked drain and run under a cold tap to stop them cooking.

3   Pat them dry with kitchen paper. Using a sharp knife cut the noodles in half (this will make them easier to eat).

4   Into a large salad bowl, add the noodles, cooked prawns, iceberg lettuce, broccoli and carrot and mix well together.

5   Drizzle the dressing over the salad and mix well. Garnish with the sesame seeds and serve.

Serves 2–4 (serves 2 as a main course and 4 as a starter)

2 bundles or portions of somen noodles

100g cooked prawns

a few handfuls of iceberg lettuce, washed and roughly chopped

100g broccoli, cut into small florets and blanched

1 small carrot, peeled and cut julienne style

black sesame seeds to garnish

Dressing

1–2 tablespoons miso paste, depending on strength

2 tablespoons lemon juice

2 teaspoons sesame oil

4 tablespoons vegetable oil

2 tablespoons water

2 teaspoons grated ginger

¼ teaspoon sugar

pepper to season

udon noodles & pork meatballs

If I'm completely honest, this recipe came about with a little luck using ingredients I had at home to make a last-minute lunch. Generally dumplings would be added to this type of noodle dish, but the meatballs work really well.

Serves 4

4 bundles or portions of udon noodles

vegetable oil

1 spring onion to garnish

shichimi togarashi and/or chilli oil to garnish

For the broth

1 litre chicken stock (see recipe on page 154)

4 tablespoons soy sauce

2 tablespoons sake

salt and pepper to season

For the meatballs

2 tablespoons soy sauce

2 tablespoons sake

1 egg

salt and pepper to season

50g panko

250g good quality pork mince

For the toppings

100g pak choi leaves, washed and roughly chopped

1 medium carrot, peeled and cut julienne style

4 eggs, hard-boiled, de-shelled and halved

1   Pour the chicken stock into a large saucepan, bring to the boil and then reduce to a simmer. Add the soy sauce and sake, and season. Mix well and reduce to a very low simmer.

2   Meanwhile, for the meatballs, in a large bowl, mix the soy sauce, sake, egg, salt and pepper together. Then add the panko and pork mince. Using your hands mix well together.

3   To make the meatballs, measure out a heaped teaspoon of minced pork mix. Then, using dampened hands, roll into the shape of a small meatball. This should make about twenty-five meatballs, depending on the size.

4   Heat some oil in a heavy-based pan on a medium heat. Place the meatballs into the hot pan and cook, turning every few minutes until they are browned on all sides.

5   Cook the udon noodles according to the pack instructions. Then toss into the broth, bring back to the boil and then immediately reduce to a simmer again.

6   Divide the udon noodles and broth between four bowls, and add the meatballs, raw vegetables and eggs if using.

7   Finally garnish with finely sliced spring onion and shichimi togarashi or chilli oil.

SUSHI & SASHIMI

When people are asked about Japanese food, sushi usually comes to mind! However, while living with my homestay family in Japan I quickly realised that sushi or sashimi wasn't featuring on the menu at all. Later I learned that, while sushi is an important part of Japan's food and culture, Japanese people tend to eat sushi out and rarely make it at home themselves!

It was from my mother-in-law Hiroko that I learned how to make sushi and fell in love with the art of sushi making. I believe the secret to great sushi is patience, along with well-prepared sushi rice, good-quality ingredients and, of course, a little skill with a sushi mat. This chapter will teach you the basics of sushi making in an easy-to-follow and relaxed style.

I love making sushi at home as it's guaranteed to be really fresh and, compared to eating sushi in restaurants, it's relatively cheap to make once you have invested in the basic ingredients.

If you're a little apprehensive about sushi rolling, start off with the temaki roll on page 175 and the gunkan roll on page 187 to build your confidence. Then move onto the other rolls once you've become familiar with how to make the sushi rice and blend the ingredients.

If you have an interest in sushi and Japanese food culture I'd recommend watching a movie called *Jiro Dreams of Sushi*. It tells the story of a Japanese sushi chef's dedication to his work and the element of 'kaizen' (continuous improvement) in Japanese culture.

The sushi recipes in this chapter are great for wowing your guests when entertaining at home, but they can also be used for packed lunches, picnics or meals at home.

sushi & sashimi Q & A

What's the difference between sushi and sashimi?

Sashimi is thinly sliced raw fish served without rice.
Sushi includes various types of sushi rolls that use sushi rice, seaweed
and different ingredients used inside the roll. There are also types of
sushi that don't use seaweed, such as nigiri (see page 188).

Is it true that sushi is raw fish?

Both cooked and raw fish can be used to make sushi. Furthermore,
you can make sushi without using fish and instead use ingredients such
as meat, fruit or vegetables.

Where can I source raw fish suitable for sashimi or sushi making?

Go to a reliable fishmonger and ask for 'sashimi-grade' fish or tell the
fishmonger that you want fish that can be eaten raw. Sashimi-grade
fish is essentially fish that is fresh enough to be eaten raw, so it's super
fresh.

How can I tell if fish is fresh?

Really fresh fish should smell of the sea and not fishy or unpleasant;
the eyes of the fish should be clear not cloudy; the skin of the fish
should be firm and shiny; if you lift the gills and look under them they
should be bright red. Whole fish will always stay fresher for longer. If
you don't fancy cleaning and filleting the fish at home, ask your fishmonger to do it for you.

What is sushi rice: 'sushi meshi'?

Sushi rice is Japanese cooked rice seasoned with sushi vinegar. Sushi
rice was traditionally made to preserve the rice and is now used to
make all types of sushi. See how to prepare sushi rice on page 172.

What's all the fuss about sushi?

I think people have a certain respect and appreciation for sushi due to the fact that it takes ten years to become a sushi chef, with the first few years dedicated to learning how to wash and cook the rice. People are also fascinated by how beautiful it looks and tastes.

What do I need to make sushi at home?

A sushi mat, Japanese white rice (you cannot make sushi with other types of rice), sushi seasoning, roasted nori seaweed sheets, a water bowl and a damp cloth.

What is nori?

Nori is a type of seaweed that is made into dry roasted seaweed sheets to make sushi rolls. It's also sold milled and this is used to sprinkle on dishes just before serving. When you open a pack of nori sheets they should be dry and crispy. Once nori is exposed to air it will become damp and soft so it's important to store it in an airtight container.

What should I serve with sushi?

Pickled ginger called 'gari', wasabi and soy sauce (be careful not to overpower the fresh flavours of the sushi with too much soy sauce and/or wasabi).

What's the difference between 'sushi' and 'zushi'?

There is no difference except that the word 'sushi' changes to 'zushi' when added to certain words. It still means the same thing.

irish salmon sashimi

Sashimi is typically served with pickled ginger, soy sauce and wasabi. The pickled ginger helps to cleanse the palate. If the fish is really fresh it should be so soft it will nearly melt in your mouth.

1   If you don't want to clean and fillet a whole salmon from scratch, then a good fishmonger will be able to give you a side of salmon instead. You can ask him to remove the pin bones and the skin if you don't feel confident doing this at home.

2   Divide the salmon into blocks (about 1 inch high and 3 inches wide).

3   Using a sharp knife thinly slice the salmon (try to cut in one clean stroke to avoid damaging the salmon).

4   Serve on a plate along with pickled ginger, soy sauce and wasabi.

Serves 2

150g sashimi-grade salmon

pickled ginger to serve

soy sauce to serve

wasabi to serve

You'll need

a sharp knife

how to prepare sushi meshi
sushi rice

A wooden bowl with a flat base called a 'hangiri' is traditionally used to make sushi rice. These can be bought online. However, you can use a pyrex dish with a flat base instead.

Serves 4

2 cups Japanese rice (using a measured rice cup this weighs 320g) uncooked

100ml Japanese rice vinegar

2 tablespoons sugar

½ teaspoon salt

wash and cook the japanese white rice

See page 32.

make the sushi vinegar

You can use ready-made sushi vinegar which is available in large supermarkets or make this from scratch:

Combine the rice vinegar and sugar in a non-aluminium saucepan and dissolve over a medium heat for a few minutes (avoid boiling). Stir in the salt, take off the heat and allow to cool.

season the rice

Transfer the hot cooked rice to a shallow pyrex dish with a flat base. Sprinkle the cooled sushi vinegar evenly over the rice and use a rice spatula to fold and turn the rice covering each grain in the sushi vinegar. Do this gently and take care not to break the rice grains.

Use a fan or a piece of cardboard to fan the rice to cool it to room temperature as quickly as possible and absorb the excess sushi vinegar.

If you're not using the sushi rice immediately then cover it with a damp cloth and store in a cool place (avoid putting it in the fridge as this will harden the rice and ideally sushi rice should be served at room temperature).

✱ Note

For all of the sushi recipes I'm using the sushi rice measurements outlined here. For the temaki, hosomaki and uramaki recipes there will be leftover rice, which you can use to make gunkan and nigiri.

temaki
sushi hand roll

This is one of the most basic types of sushi rolls and takes little time to prepare. If you're a novice to sushi making I'd recommend you start with this cone-shaped roll, as it will help build your confidence with the slightly more complicated rolls.

1   Mix the smoked trout, avocado cubes and cream cheese in a bowl together. Set aside.

2   To halve a nori sheet, place it in front of you with the lines running vertically. Hold the top of the nori sheet and fold it in half. Gently press on the sheet and then it should easily pull apart into two halves.

3   Lay half a sheet of nori shiny-side down. Place the water bowl and damp cloth nearby. Put a heaped tablespoon (60g) of sushi rice on the left side of the nori sheet. Use moistened fingertips (using the water bowl) to spread the rice evenly over nearly half of the nori sheet (see a–b). Use the water bowl and damp cloth to remove rice from your fingers.

4   Place a few lettuce leaves at a 45 degree angle on the rice. Then carefully place some of the smoked trout mix on top of the lettuce (try not to overload with ingredients as this will make it difficult to roll) (see c–d).

5   Carefully roll the temaki by folding the bottom left corner of the nori towards the top right corner of the rice. Continue to fold and place a few grains of cooked rice on the final corner of the nori to complete and hold the fold (see e–g).

6   Fill the temaki with another spoonful of the smoked trout mix. Garnish with a spoonful of caviar or mixed sesame seeds (see h). Make seven more temaki rolls in the same way.

Makes 8 temaki
(serves 4)

sushi rice (see page 172)

For the temaki filling
200g goatsbridge smoked trout, chopped into small pieces

2 ripened avocados, cut into small cubes (drizzled in lemon juice to avoid browning)

200g cream cheese

4 nori sheets, halved

2 handfuls of lamb's lettuce, washed and dried

Goatsbridge trout caviar or mixed sesame seeds to garnish

You'll need
a water bowl

a damp clean cloth

hosomaki

thin sushi roll

I like this type of roll because it has only one ingredient inside, allowing you to enjoy the taste of the rice, seaweed and inside ingredient all in one mouthful.

Makes 8 rolls (serves 4)

sushi rice (see page 172)

4 nori sheets, halved

possible fillings (I've listed my favourite for this type of roll). All the ingredients should be cut into thin long strips.

- blanched asparagus
- ripened avocado, coated in fresh lemon juice to avoid browning
- ripened mango
- cucumber
- smoked trout
- raw salmon/tuna
- cooked chicken strips

soy sauce to serve

wasabi to serve

pickled ginger to serve

You'll need

a sushi mat

a small water bowl

a damp clean cloth

a sharp knife

1. Place half a sheet of nori shiny-side down with the lines in the nori running vertical on a sushi mat.

2. Dip your fingertips in the water bowl and shake off any excess water.

3. Take a large spoonful of rice (80g) and using your fingertips gently spread the rice over the nori sheet trying not to press on the rice too hard. Spread the rice to the edges of the nori, leaving a 2cm gap at the top of the seaweed (see a).

4. Place the ingredients in a straight line on the nori sheet. Hold the nearest end of the mat with your index fingers and thumbs. Use the rest of your fingers to hold the ingredients in place. Roll the mat forward to bring the nori and rice wrap around the fillings. Press down firmly but gently to create a roll shape (see b–d).

5. To finish the roll, pull the end of the mat with one hand and continue to push the roll forward with the other hand (see e).

6. Place the roll on a chopping board and using a sharp knife cut in half (try to cut only in one direction; see f). Then, using a damp clean cloth, wipe the knife clean and continue to cut the two halves into four pieces and then cut the four pieces in half, which leaves you with eight pieces altogether.

7. Make seven more rolls in the same way. Each serving should consist of sixteen pieces. Serve with soy sauce, wasabi and pickled ginger.

nigiri

Gunkan

hosomaki'

Uramaki

uramaki
inside-out sushi roll

This is visually the most impressive sushi roll as the rice is on the outside of the roll, which can be decorated with sesame seeds or even chopped dill. I always drizzle the apples with lemon juice to avoid browning.

Makes 4 rolls (serves 4)

sushi rice (see page 172)

2 nori sheets, halved

1–2 teaspoons mixed sesame seeds or home-made furikake
(see page 36; chopped dill could also be used)

For the sushi filling

140g good quality cooked crab meat

½ tablespoon crème fraîche

pea-size dollop of wasabi paste

2 apples, cut into thin strips

1 roasted red pepper, cut into thin strips

You'll need

2 sushi mats

cling film

a small water bowl

a damp clean cloth

a sharp knife

1   Wrap one sushi mat in cling film to prevent the rice sticking in point 3. Prepare a small bowl of water and a clean damp cloth – you'll need these while you're rolling the sushi.

2   Lay half a sheet of nori on a sushi mat (use the sushi mat with no cling film), shiny-side down and with the lines in the nori running vertically. Place a quarter of the sushi rice on the nori (100g). Use lightly moistened fingertips to gently spread the rice evenly over the nori sheet, and then sprinkle over the sesame seeds or furikake (see a–b overleaf).

3   Place the second sushi mat over the rice and press firmly but gently to secure the rice onto the nori sheet. Flip the sushi mats around so the mat originally facing up is now facing down and remove the top mat. The rice should be facing down and the nori facing up (see c–e). Set aside while you prepare the fillings.

4   In a small bowl mix together the crab meat, crème fraîche and wasabi. Then, place all the ingredients (i.e. the crab-meat mix, apple and red pepper) in a straight line on the nori sheet. Hold the nearest end of the mat with your index fingers and thumbs. Use the rest of your fingers to hold the ingredients in place. Roll the mat forward to bring the nori and rice wrap around the fillings. Press down firmly but gently to create a roll shape (see f–g).

5   To finish the roll, pull the end of the mat with one hand and continue to push the roll forward with the other hand (if some ingredients fall out the sides simply push them back in and don't worry if the edges of the roll look untidy). Wrap the mat around the sushi roll to form a secure roll shape. Detach the cling film from the mat and wrap around the roll to secure it when cutting (see h).

6   Transfer the cling film-wrapped roll to a chopping board and cut in half with a sharp knife. Wipe the knife clean with a damp cloth and continue to halve each piece until you have eight pieces. Remove the cling film before transferring to a serving plate.

7   Make three more rolls in the same way. Serve with pickled ginger, wasabi and soy sauce.

chirashi-zushi
scattered sushi

This is a type of sushi where the sushi rice is served in a bowl or on a large serving dish with a variety of ingredients mixed through the rice and also on top of the rice, including beautiful yellow ribbons which are made from egg by simply frying it like a crêpe and then cutting it into thin ribbons. Although sushi is usually not made in Japanese homes, this is one exception, most likely because no rolling is required for this type of sushi. It's served in homes across Japan to celebrate the New Year and other special occasions.

Serves 4–6

sushi rice (see page 172)

vegetable oil

sesame oil and soy sauce to serve

black sesame seeds to garnish

For the sushi fillings and toppings

2 eggs, beaten

½ yellow pepper and ½ red pepper, cut into small cubes

1 avocado, cut into small cubes

8 large prawns, cut into bite-size pieces

1   To make the egg crêpe for the yellow ribbons to decorate the top of the sushi rice, lightly oil a non-stick frying pan with vegetable oil and place on a medium to high heat. Depending on the size of your pan, place about half the beaten egg on the frying pan so you have a very thin layer of egg like a crêpe. Now adjust the heat to low and leave the egg on the pan until the edges of the egg crêpe start to break away from the pan. Transfer to a large plate and set aside. Continue to do this until all the beaten egg is cooked. Place the egg crêpes on top of each other as they are cooked. When you're finished, roll the pile of egg crêpes together. Then using a sharp knife cut into thin ribbons.

2   Allow the seasoned sushi rice to cool to room temperature, and then mix half of the peppers, avocado and prawns into the rice. Place in a large serving dish.

3   Scatter the remaining ingredients on top of the rice mix including the egg ribbons.

4   For extra flavour lightly drizzle sesame oil and soy sauce all over and garnish with sesame seeds.

✳   Tip

I like to top this with a few extra whole prawns.

gunkan
japanese warship sushi

Gunkan translates as 'Japanese warship sushi' because the shape and appearance of this particular type of sushi resembles a Japanese warship. It is most often decorated with different types of fish eggs. I think this is the most visually impressive sushi roll with the least rolling effort and skill required. I usually make this type of sushi roll to use up rice and seaweed left over from making the other sushi rolls.

1   Moisten your hands in the water bowl, shaking off any excess water. Take a small ball of sushi rice (25g) and place on the palm of your hand. Using a firm but gentle squeeze, mould into an oval-shaped rice ball (see a).

2   Wrap the nori around the rice with the shiny side of the nori facing out. Use a spare rice grain to seal the end of the nori. The nori should be higher than the rice to allow room for the topping (see b–c).

3   Using your finger, smear a thin line of wasabi on the top of the rice (this is optional).

4   Place your preferred topping on top of the rice so that it sits slightly above the level of the nori (see d).

5   Serve on a plate with soy sauce, wasabi and pickled ginger.

use leftover sushi rice or go to page 172 to see how to make sushi rice

nori strips, 3cm tall

wasabi (optional)

soy sauce to serve

pickled ginger to serve

Topping options

- Goatsbridge trout caviar (or any type of fish egg locally available)

- mango, peeled and chopped into tiny cubes

- avocado, peeled and chopped into tiny cubes

You'll need

a water bowl

a damp clean cloth

✱ Tip

Use the damp cloth to remove excess water or lose rice grains from your hands.

nigiri
moulded sushi

Nigiri is a type of sushi made with a small ball of sushi rice and topped with a thin slice of fish, meat or vegetable. Depending on the topping used, a thin piece of nori can be wrapped around the topping and the rice ball to secure the nigiri. It's usually served in pairs.

use leftover sushi rice or go to page 172 to see how to make sushi rice

wasabi

soy sauce to serve

pickled ginger to serve

Topping options

- thinly sliced raw fish or pickled fish

- cooked or raw prawns

- roasted red pepper slices

- thinly sliced cooked chicken breast or beef

- avocado slices

You'll need

a water bowl

a damp clean cloth

1   Moisten your hands in the water bowl, shaking off any excess water. Take a small ball of sushi rice (25g) and place on the palm of your hand. Using a firm but gentle squeeze, mould into an oval-shaped rice ball (see a).

2   Use your index finger to put a spot of wasabi on the top of the rice (see b).

3   Place the topping on the rice ball (see c).

4   Place your thumb along the base of the rice to help flatten slightly so it will sit securely on a flat surface.

5   Serve with soy sauce, wasabi and pickled ginger.

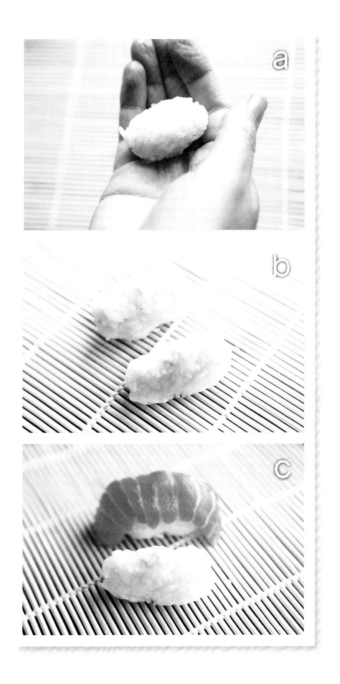

DESSERTS & DRINKS

Desserts aren't a key feature in a Japanese meal although sometimes fruit may be served at the end of a meal. However modern Japan is influenced by the West and classic French desserts are very popular. Many Japanese chefs travel to France to learn how to make desserts and then return to open their own bakeries. One thing that I noticed when I returned to Ireland after living in Japan is that portion sizes of desserts in Japan tend to be much smaller than here in the West.

There is a type of traditional Japanese dessert called 'wagashi' which uses ingredients such as rice and azuki beans. The ingredients used and the presentation of wagashi are closely connected to nature and the seasons. For example, in springtime you'll see many cherry-blossom-flavoured wagashi. These are eaten as a special treat with green tea in the afternoon like a snack. When Japanese people go to visit another part of Japan it is customary to bring back a souvenir from that town called 'omiyage'. The most popular type of omiyage are these pretty little Japanese wagashi cakes.

Matcha (powdered green tea) is one Japanese ingredient that is often used in baking. I've included my matcha swiss roll recipe and matcha ice-cream recipe in this chapter for you to try at home. I've also included one of Japan's most loved fruits, 'kaki', better known as persimmon fruit here in the West.

matcha

powdered green tea

I was first introduced to matcha at a traditional Japanese tea ceremony in Japan. During the ceremony a large bowl of matcha was prepared by the tea master and passed around. I have to mention that matcha prepared at traditional tea ceremonies is very concentrated, especially for someone who has never tasted it before. I'll never forget the strong and bitter taste of the matcha and pretending to like it as my homestay mother observed my reaction to this nearly sacred drink! The matcha that I make at home and find served outside of Japan is not as concentrated, so it's easier to drink, and you acquire a taste for it over time.

Matcha is becoming a super drink here in the West due to its health benefits, such as aiding weight loss, aiding digestion, relieving stress and anxiety, boosting energy levels, controlling food cravings and because of its high levels of antioxidants. Remember though that it needs to be drunk in moderation, so a few cups a day is plenty.

Matcha is not widely available in supermarkets but it can be found in Asian speciality stores, some health stores or online. I've listed one of my favourite stockists at the back of this book. They stock 'ingredient matcha' which is suitable for baking and costs about half the price of drinking matcha. You can use drinking matcha for baking, but it will work out more expensive.

How to make matcha

1 Put a quarter of a teaspoon of green-tea powder into a cup.

2 Use a bamboo whisk (called a 'chasen') or small metal whisk to get rid of any lumps in the powder.

3 Leave water just boiled in a kettle aside for a few minutes to reduce the temperature of the water to below boiling point.

4 Pour a small amount of the hot water into the cup and use the whisk to mix the water and green tea powder together until all the lumps are dissolved.

5 Fill the cup with more hot water and serve (add more or less water depending on whether you want a weak or a strong cup of tea).

matcha swiss roll

1   Preheat a fan oven to 180°C.

2   Whisk the eggs and caster sugar in an electric mixer for about 10 minutes until nice and fluffy.

3   Sieve the flour and matcha together a few times to make sure the matcha powder is completely mixed into the flour.

4   Using a large spoon gently fold the sieved flour into the egg and sugar mix.

5   Carefully line a baking tin with greaseproof paper and lightly grease with butter.

6   Pour the batter into the baking tin, using a spatula to gently even it out.

7   Bake in the oven for 10 to 15 minutes or until a skewer/sharp knife inserted comes out clean.

8   Remove from the oven and allow to cool for a few minutes in the baking tin.

9   Turn the cake over onto a clean tea towel, then carefully peel off the greaseproof paper.

10 Roll the cake in the tea towel and allow to cool (this will avoid it breaking later).

11 Unfold the cake when it is cool and spread the whipped cream evenly on the cake.

12 Roll again and dust with icing sugar. Put in the fridge until ready to eat.

Serves 8

4 eggs, at room temperature

100g caster sugar

100g plain flour

1 tablespoon ingredient matcha powder (see supplier and stockists on page 216)

250ml whipped cream for filling

icing sugar for dusting

You'll need

swiss roll tin
(10" x 15" or 13" x 9")

quick & easy
matcha ice cream

You don't need an ice-cream maker for this recipe and it takes about five minutes to make. So give it a try and I'm sure you'll be experimenting with different flavoured ice creams once you see first-hand the rewards of making your own.

Serves 8

2 tablespoons ingredient matcha powder, mixed with about 4 tablespoons water

500ml double cream

300ml condensed milk

1 tablespoon lemon juice

1   Using a fork or a small whisk, mix the matcha powder and water together until all lumps are dissolved. Set aside.

2   Whip the cream until soft peaks form.

3   Stir in the condensed milk, lemon juice and matcha mix using a large spoon. Mix well together.

4   Transfer the ice cream into an airtight container and freeze for at least 4 hours or overnight.

✳   Note

See supplier and stockist list on page 216 for ingredient matcha powder.

melon & pomegranate fruit salad

Ginger is an essential ingredient in Japanese savoury cooking, but it also adds a refreshing flavour to the syrup to flavour this simple fruit salad.

1   Place all the ingredients for the syrup in a saucepan and bring to the boil. Immediately reduce to a simmer for about 10 minutes. Take off the heat and set aside to cool. Once cooled, remove the ginger pieces from the syrup (these can be added later as a topping to the salad if you like).

2   Put the melon and pomegranate seeds into a large serving bowl.

3   Pour the syrup over the fruit and mix well together. Garnish with mint leaves. Serve immediately or store in the fridge.

Serves 4

1 whole honeydew melon, peeled and cut into bite-size cubes

1 pomegranate, seeds removed

mint leaves to garnish

For the syrup

90ml water

75g caster sugar

40g ginger, peeled and thinly sliced

kaki (persimmon fruit) tart

I remember collecting buckets of persimmon fruit (also called sharon fruit) with the elementary school children behind the local school where I worked in Japan. It reminded me of how we pick apples here in Ireland. In the past few years I was delighted to see this beautifully coloured fruit in my local supermarket. It is best eaten ripe otherwise it will be hard and bitter. To check if it's ripe just press on the skin and it should be soft to touch. A really ripe persimmon can be eaten by slicing the top off the fruit and scooping out the flesh with a spoon. The persimmon and white chocolate cream in this recipe are a marriage made in heaven!

Serves 9

puff pastry, shop bought and pre-rolled (320g puff pastry makes 9 servings)

5 persimmon fruit (about half a persimmon fruit per serving),

brown sugar to dust

100g good quality white chocolate

250ml fresh cream, whipped

icing sugar to serve

1   Unwrap the pastry and roll out on a chopping board. Using a sharp knife cut the pastry into rectangular pieces large enough to serve one person for dessert. For 320g of puff pastry I divided the pastry into nine servings.

2   Peel the persimmon fruit, cut in half and then into thick slices.

3   Place four or five pieces along the centre of the pastry. Dust with brown sugar.

4   Bake at 200°C in a fan oven for 10–15 minutes until the pastry is slightly browned and crisp.

5   Break the white chocolate into small squares and place in a glass bowl over a saucepan of boiling water on a medium heat. Allow the chocolate to slowly melt while stirring.

6   Once completely melted set aside for a few minutes to let cool a little, then add to the whipped cream and mix well together.

7   Serve the persimmon tart with a spoonful of white chocolate cream and dust with icing sugar.

sake cosmopolitan

Sake is an integral part of Japanese cuisine in the same way as wine is to French cuisine. It's traditionally drunk from small cups called 'choko' and can be served either hot or cold. It's a popular option for cocktails and has a lower alcohol content than vodka. Asian speciality stores now stock a decent selection of sake, including sparkling sake.

1   Fill a cocktail shaker with ice, then add all the liquid ingredients and mix well together until well chilled.

2   Serve in a cocktail/martini glass and garnish with mint leaves.

Makes 2 cocktails

90ml sake

30ml Cointreau

30ml lime juice

90ml cranberry juice

mint leaves to garnish

BENTO PLANNER

One of the things I was most intrigued about when I moved to Japan was its bento culture. I was astonished by the amount of effort that Japanese people put into their packed lunches. My Japanese friend once told me that they look forward to their bento all day and opening it is a pleasant surprise or treat. It wasn't long before I was completely immersed in this bento culture and looked forward to making my own bento every night for work the following day.

A typical Japanese bento will have something from each of the food groups, including carbohydrates such as rice, noodles or bread; meat or fish; and vegetables and fruit. Since the bento box is divided into different compartments, various dishes can be stored in the box together, giving a nutritionally balanced meal which looks appealing.

Japanese parents tend to make their children's bento very animated and colourful. There are simple ways to do this, like using a cookie cutter to make vegetables and fruit into different shapes such as flowers or stars.

Apart from the standard packed-lunch-type bento, there is also the bento that is served in Japanese restaurants and gives the customer a taste of a few different dishes at one time. These restaurant bentos are very popular outside Japan and reasonably priced.

In this chapter I'm going to provide a variety of bento menu options using recipes taken from this book. The bento menu options can be served at home to your family or while entertaining guests. They can also be used as packed lunches or for picnics.

ebi furai bento

Protein – ebi furai (page 120) with lemon wedges and mayonnaise dip

Carbohydrate – boiled rice (page 32) with furikake sprinkle (page 36)

Vegetable – cucumber and carrot sticks or shapes

Fresh fruit – mandarin

yakisoba bento

Protein – boiled egg

Carbohydrate and vegetables – yakisoba (page 158) topped with beni shoga

Fresh fruit – melon slices and/or raspberries

chicken gyoza bento

Protein – chicken gyoza with dipping sauce (page 83)

Carbohydrate – onigiri/rice balls (page 37)

Vegetables – salted edamame (page 131)

Fruit – apple wedges

chicken katsu curry bento

Protein – chicken katsu curry (page 91) on a bed of lettuce topped with beni shoga

Carbohydrate - boiled rice (page 32)

Vegetable – steamed broccoli and cherry tomatoes

Fresh fruit – mango cubes

sushi bento

Protein and carbohydrate – selection of sushi with soy sauce and wasabi (pages 175–188)

Vegetable – pickled salad (page 150)

Fruit – sliced kiwi

salmon teriyaki bento

Protein – salmon teriyaki with sesame sprinkles (page 116)

Carbohydrate – boiled rice (page 32)

Vegetable – blanched spinach

Fruit – pineapple slices

suppliers & stockists

Asian Market

Asian speciality store

www.asiamarket.ie

Tel: +353 (0) 1 6779764

Oriental Emporium

Asian speciality store

www.orientalemporium.ie

Tel: +353 (0) 1 2572218

Avoca

Foodhall and health food section

www.avoca.ie

Tel: +353 (0) 1 2746900

Koyu Matcha

Japanese powdered tea and utensils

http://koyumatcha.com

Tel: +353 (0) 1 6190295

James Whelan

Butcher and supplier of Wagyu beef

www.jameswhelanbutchers.com

Tel: +353 (0) 52 6182477

Palais des Thes

Japanese tea and utensils

www.palaisdesthes.com

Tel: +353 (0) 1 6708752

Sea of Vitality

Irish seaweed products

http://seaofvitality.ie

Tel: +353 (0) 86 2324270

Wild Irish Sea Veg

Irish seaweed products

http://wildirishseaveg.com

Tel: +353 (0) 87 0922555

Goatsbridge Trout

Irish trout products including caviar

http://goatsbridgetrout.ie/

Tel: +353 (0) 86 818 8340

conversion tables

temperature conversion table

Fan Oven	Conventional Oven	Gas Mark	Fahrenheit
90°C (very cool)	110°C	¼	225°F
110°C	130°C	½	266°F
120°C (cool)	140°C	1	284°F
130°C	150°C	2	302°F
140°C (moderate)	160°C	3	320°F
150°C	170°C	3	338°F
160°C	180°C	4	356°F
170°C (mod. hot)	190°C	5	374°F
180°C	200°C	6	392°F
190°C	210°C	6	410°F
200°C (hot)	220°C	7	428°F
210°C	230°C	8	450°F
220°C (very hot)	240°C	9	464°F

dry ingredients

Metric	Imperial
5 grams	⅛ ounce
10g	¼oz
15g	½oz
20g	¾oz
25g	1oz
50g	2oz
75g	3oz
100–125g	4oz
150g	5oz
175g	6oz
200g	7oz
225g	8oz
250g	9oz
275g	10oz
300g	11oz
325g	12oz
350g	13oz
400g	14oz
425g	15oz
450g	1lb
1kg	2¼lb

liquids

Metric	Imperial
25ml	1 fluid ounce
50ml	2 fluid ounces
75ml	3 fluid ounces
125ml	4 fluid ounces
150ml	5 fluid ounces
175ml	6 fluid ounces
200ml	7 fluid ounces
225ml	8 fluid ounces
250ml	9 fluid ounces
275ml	10 fluid ounces
500ml	17 fluid ounces
1 litre	1.75 pints
American cup	8 fluid ounces
small glass	5 fluid ounces

index

MERCIER PRESS

Cork

www.mercierpress.ie

© Fiona Uyema, 2015

Photography by a Fox in the Kitchen

Food Styling by Orla Neligan of Cornershop Productions

www.cornershopproductions.com

Assisted by Aga Wypych

ISBN: 978 1 78117 334 3

10 9 8 7 6 5 4 3 2 1

PROPS: **Avoca:** HQ Kilmacanogue, Bray, Co. Wicklow. **T:** (01) 2746939; **E:** info@avoca.ie; www.avoca.ie | **Meadows & Byrne:** Dublin, Cork, Galway, Clare, Tipperary. **T:** (01) 2804554/(021) 4344100; **E:** info@meadowsandbyrne.ie; www.meadowsandbyrne.com | **Marks & Spencer:** Unit 1–28, Dundrum Town Centre, Dublin 16. **T:** 01 299 1300; **W:** www.marksandspencer.ie | **Article Dublin:** Powerscourt Townhouse, South William Street, Dublin 2. **T:** 01 6799268; **E:** items@articledublin.com; **W:** www.articledublin.com | **House of Fraser:** Dundrum Town Centre, Dublin 16. **T:** 01 2991400; **E:** dundrum@hof.co.uk; **W:** www.houseoffraser.co.uk | **Dunnes Stores:** 46–50 South Great Georges Street, Dublin 2. **T:** 1890 253185; www.dunnesstores.com | **Harold's Bazaar:** 208 Harold's Cross Road, Dublin 6W. **T:** 087 7228789. | **Historic Interiors:** Oberstown, Lusk, Co. Dublin. **T:** 01 8437174; **E:** killian@historicinteriors.net | **Homebase:** Nutgrove Retail Park, Nutgrove Avenue, Dublin 14. **T:** 01 4916118; **W:** www.homebase.co.uk | **TK Maxx:** The Park, Carrickmines, Dublin 18. **T:** 01 2074798; **W:** www.tkmaxx.ie | **Bakers Bling on Etsy:** www.etsy.com/shop/BakersBlingShop

Printed and bound in the EU.